THE
RETURN VOYAGE

95,000 Miles
on the Paths of Our Ancestors

Inette Miller

To Charles:
What a wonderful organization!
Inspiring!
Aloha.
Inette Miller

∞ INFINITY
PUBLISHING

Copyright © 2013 by Inette Miller

Cover Design:
  Cathi Stevenson
Front Cover Sculpture and Back Cover Photograph:
  Marlene Keller Czajkowski
Photo of 'Iokepa at Waimea Canyon:
  Jeremy Orbe-Smith
Photo of Inette over ocean:
  Ron Czajkowski
Photo of crowd scene:
  Hamilton Gregory
Photo of Inette and 'Iokepa seated:
  Danny Hashimoto

ISBN 978-0-7414-9830-4 Paperback
ISBN 978-0-7414-9831-1 Hardcover
ISBN 978-0-7414-9832-8 eBook

Printed in the United States of America

Published October 2013

INFINITY PUBLISHING
1094 New DeHaven Street, Suite 100
West Conshohocken, PA 19428-2713
Toll-free (877) BUY BOOK
Local Phone (610) 941-9999
Fax (610) 941-9959
Info@buybooksontheweb.com
www.buybooksontheweb.com

To Phil Williams, Ho'okani Pū

CONTENTS

An Aside

Quite intentionally, these stories are not arranged chronologically. They are ordered, instead, for an understanding of the larger themes. However, the book invites either sequential reading of the stories, or dipping into its pieces where intuition or mood strikes.

Many of the stories have been adapted from those that appeared earlier on the Ever Changing Page of our website: www.ReturnVoyage.com. You are invited to follow those pages and discover with us what comes next.

Scenic Overview

It's been almost sixteen years since our outrageously dissimilar paths first crossed on a small island at the northwest corner of the Hawaiian chain in the middle of the Pacific. 'Iokepa and I were married there four years later.

If you are fond of numbers (I struggle to remember even my zip code): we were married on the twelfth day of the twelfth month at noon, nearly twelve years ago. For Native Hawaiians, noon is the most potent moment of the day; when male and female merge their independent strengths and energy.

We were well-met. These many years later – with my perfect twenty-twenty hindsight – I'm aware that this has been an extraordinary journey we've chosen to take together.

'Iokepa's recent Hallmark anniversary card to me read: "Someday, many years from now, we'll look back on this crazy time in our life together and wonder how we did it all. We'll look at each other and say: 'I'd do it all again.' There's no one I'd rather go through life with than you."

I handed him mine. Mine had the added Hallmark inducement of musical accompaniment: Billy Joel sang, "For the Longest Time."

Please stick with me; I promise that this will not be a sentimental tribute to the perfectibility of marriage – or to the wonders of this particular one.

In Retrospect

I was on a ten-day vacation in Hawai'i, when I met this handsome brown-skinned, powerfully-built man with a head of startling silver hair. It was sunrise Christmas morning at an ancient Hawaiian *heiau*, or sacred site. I'd been a journalist, author, and writing workshop teacher all of my adult life, a single mother for thirteen years. I lived in Portland, Oregon. I was fifty-one years old.

He'd been a successful businessman – paving freeways, laying waterlines for Seattle and environs.

Ten months before we met he'd had a spiritual epiphany that demanded (in the presence of his long-dead grandmothers) that he relinquish everything he'd worked for all his life (considerable) and reclaim his aboriginal heritage (at that time, obscure) – and thus fulfill the promises he'd made when he took on life: his destiny.

'Iokepa was to relinquish a life of obsessively hard work and of profound pleasure, of money and travel and expensive toys, to assume the mantle of responsibility for his grievously oppressed and denigrated aboriginal Hawaiian people. Neither he nor I understood the breadth of that responsibility, or that surrender.

In two weeks he did just that and returned to his ancestral roots in Hawai'i. He lived there without income, credit card, or identification that claimed other than his Native Hawaiian ancestry. It was to be a walk of faith and the beginning of what his ancestors called, his "ten-year grooming." His lifework was directed toward the fulfillment of a 1000-year-old prophecy that foresaw the resurrection of his aboriginal culture as the beacon to a needy world.

Just ten months after his life-changing epiphany, we met. Six months later, my sons and I left our impressive hilltop home in Portland and moved to Hawai'i. We joined lives with 'Iokepa.

With no home, we lived on sand beaches in fourteen tents and on twelve air mattresses over the next ten years. Everything we owned fit into the trunk of my increasingly aged Camry and a very small storage closet. We often went hungry. Life had become very simple – and very complex.

We lived among homeless addicts of every ethnicity. We lived as an alternative – with integrity and responsibility – in the manner of 'Iokepa's ancestors, the Native Hawaiian people.

Those years were painful – every last one of them. Intellectually I'd always had empathy for the "less fortunate." It was a different story when I became one of them. It was a different story when all choices based on my superior education and opportunity evaporated. They no longer had relevance. I refuse to idealize those years; but I also refuse to renounce them.

Because of those ten years, I've come into the fullness of my own in these past six. Not my own as I lived it in Portland, for self and family and friends, but my own in the surrender to forces greater than a paycheck, and wider than the faces that I already recognize.

Huliau – The Return Voyage

Because of those ten years, 'Iokepa and I have been asked in these last six to speak words across the United States that resonate with the truth and wisdom of the aboriginal Hawaiian culture. This was a culture that refused war, violence, hierarchy, and gender segregation for more than 12,000 years. It has at least a few things to teach a 21st-century audience, who seemed to have forgotten how that might be accomplished.

In adherence to that culture, every one of our decisions, large and small, is offered up to the ancestors for guidance. We move in every breath without plan or expectation.

We tell, too, the stories of our life together. Still we have no predictable income, no home, and no identification that ties 'Iokepa to any government other than his nation of Hawai'i.

We solicit nothing. We speak only where invited. We're funded through donation bowl alone; it is how we eat and how we pay for gas. The shiny black, 1998 Camry was a gift for this purpose. We fondly dubbed it, the "Dark Horse."

We live what we speak: That when we accept and embrace our individual destiny – the work we're each put on the planet to accomplish – we are supported in unforeseeable ways. Sometimes our words and stories inspire listeners in North Carolina or New Mexico or Maine to claim their own gifts, their own destinies – fearlessly.

When the inspiration for this journey came six years ago now, the name *Huliau – the Return Voyage* was given by the ancestral Hawaiian grandmothers – and there was little doubt that they were the right words.

They spoke literally of the *kanaka maoli* (aboriginal Hawaiians), who travelled with faith and without fear the breadth of the Pacific for thousands of years in their state-of-the-art sailing canoes. They didn't have to know where the ocean currents might take them – but they would always need to know how to return home.

They travelled the seas and they plotted their return trip by the night skies. They weaved that celestial navigation into chants – their oral maps – that were handed down for generations. Their chants literally guided them home. Often, that return voyage came generations after the original voyagers set out, armed only with *aloha*. Aloha meant: In the presence of God in every breath.

'Iokepa chokes down tears when he describes the feeling of their quite literal return voyage. He "remembers" that first sight of home: the volcanic mountain from which each Island was birthed, the pristine beaches, the familiar smell of sandalwood – his Islands.

But in describing the ancestors' actual return, 'Iokepa evokes the powerful feelings that are familiar to each of us when we rediscover our true home. *Huliau – the Return Voyage* is, in this most recent incarnation, pure metaphor.

Each of our gatherings during these years, in simple and elegant homes across the country, has been a summons to return to that which we are all born knowing: our unique and universal inheritance. These, our abundant gifts, are too often surrendered to the distraction of our noisy world; abandoned to the demand of our technological toys; or dismissed as insignificant by our by-the-book-only education.

Return Voyage continues to be an empowering bellow into the wind: all we need lies within ourselves. We are – every one of us – supported on our human journey by universal ancestors who recognize the gifts we carry and the specific purpose we signed on for, and who work to foster the fulfillment of that purpose.

'Iokepa says: "*Ask*...and then *listen*. Your answers are in the wind and the rain and in every single element of creation."

For three of these six years, the Return Voyage gatherings were propagated by word of mouth. We gathered and we spoke in scores of crowded and not-so-crowded living rooms. Then, three years ago *Grandmothers Whisper* struggled to publication: scrawled for thirteen years on legal pads in a folding chair on Hawaiian beaches, occasionally in the homes of strangers.

We hauled those book boxes and that message to countless bookstores, assorted churches, a few colleges, and clubs of every imaginable diversion or pursuit. Our gatherings are always highly interactive; we stand on no platforms, speak through no microphone.

"We *all* come from indigenous peoples." 'Iokepa says. "All of our indigenous peoples understood their responsibility for one another and for the entire natural world. They had to in order to survive."

Slowly, oh so slowly, we have crisscrossed this continent eleven times. We have experienced all four seasons fully: golden oak leaves and red maples in October; a frozen Mississippi River in January; tulips, daffodils, and azalea in April; fresh green deciduous leaves budding, sprouting, and leafing in June.

All of this is exotic to me. When you've lived on these tropical Islands for any length of time, seasons are something you do not take for granted. 'Iokepa and I savored every dogwood blossom, forsythia flower, and icy snowball in these years. We'd arrived in Seattle that first winter in late December without sweaters, coats, or boots.

Each of our four speaking and book tours – ranging from eight months to more than a year – was sandwiched between much-needed respite and renewal on the Islands. We yearned always to refill on 'Iokepa's land, in his ocean, with his people – and our months there were never enough.

We spoke on our continental crossings to Native Americans, African-Americans, Hispanic, Asian, and Caucasian folk of every social and economic background. We spoke of a people who took responsibility for every thread of creation; a matriarchal culture that embraced the feminine in every man and the masculine in every woman; a people who could not fathom separation – natural or human.

Our work has been about much more than the Native Hawaiian plea for righteous sovereignty, for freedom from oppression. It is about personal and cultural freedom on every inch of this planet. The final words of *Grandmothers Whisper*:

We could not have foreseen the collapsing world economy. But we know this: security is our birthright. We do not lose our compassion, our responsibility for one another, our ability to give and receive – our very lives – unless we agree to it.

No circumstance and no person can take away what we were born with – our deep connection to every part of creation and to one another – unless we agree to surrender it.

It was at the explicit moment when those words on the page ended that our dynamic and all-embracing current journey began.

Years ago 'Iokepa's grandmothers told him: "Your imagination can't take you that far." They were exactly right.

August 2013

'IOKEPA

AND HIS PEOPLE

A Single Motion

The Prelude

'Iokepa and I lived on Hawaiian public beaches for years. We slept on the reclining seats of a seriously aging 1991 Camry when there wasn't gas enough to get us to the tent. Picnic tables were our dining room furniture; outside showers were our bathtubs; filthy public toilets were our dressing rooms and more.

For two of those years, our youngest son, then fourteen to sixteen, lived in the tent next door or on the back seat of the "Hotel Camry." He did his homework on our "dining table," took his showers before dawn, lived on peanut butter and jelly, and hitchhiked to school.

Ours was, and continues to be, a life of surrender. Both 'Iokepa and I (in quite different ways) left lives of hard work, generous recompense, and comfort.

As a result, we now know that when our hands are emptied, they will be refilled; when our spirit is drained, it will be replenished.

Often 'Iokepa has said on our speaking tours across the U.S: 'We lived this, so *you* don't have to. We lived this so we could speak to you now."

In those sandy parks among impoverished Native Hawaiian families, I learned things I'd never have learned in my big glass house built into the side of the mountain in Portland. I experienced life as I never could have experienced it surrounded by the abundance of my oriental rugs, my fine art, my finer library, and my view of the city lights below.

What I learned looked something like this. When 'Iokepa and I could afford a large bag of Krusteaz pancake mix, we served the entire park from our small frying pan. When we managed a Costco-size bag of pasta, no one went hungry. When the fisherman in the tent next door had a good day in the ocean, everyone ate fish. When the mango trees were bearing, everyone had mango juice dripping from their chins.

This had nothing to do with "barter," a word and concept that did not exist among the Hawaiian ancestors. This had only to do with the necessity of community – and their faith in absolute abundance.

When my not-yet-daughter-in-law from Nashville visited our life in the parks, she was literally stricken by the ease of the giving and the receiving. She speaks of it still.

And while very few folks are required to relinquish their material aspirations in order to live out their destiny (it is not *asked*), every single one of us is required to recognize the necessity of that flow: the giving and the receiving that the Native Hawaiians considered a single motion. All of us give; all of us receive; neither motion is more holy. None of us get to opt out of the circle.

The Story

A few weeks ago we spoke at a wondrous gathering in Sarasota, Florida. The tiny bungalow was packed with an energy and excitement that I would have loved to bottle and take with me. Remarkably, it turns out, we actually did.

After 'Iokepa and I shared our stories in this crowded living room, an engaging woman of our age contributed hers. Patricia bubbled over her eagerness to tell: "Here's what happened to me!"

That very morning, Patricia had gone out to breakfast. As she settled into her booth at the restaurant, she realized that she'd forgotten her wallet. All she had was her change purse. The waitress approached to take her order, and Patricia said, "I'll take a moment to order; I have to count my change. I left my wallet at home."

She figured that she had just enough for a bowl of oatmeal. The waitress returned and said this: "The man at that table offered, 'Tell her to order whatever she wants. I'll pay.'"

Patricia's first response was to refuse. Her second response was, "Why I think I *will*." She proceeded to order: "Two eggs over easy, hash browns, bacon, and whole wheat toast." At the end of the meal she thanked her benefactor and told his wife, "What a wonderful husband you have."

From where I sat in the living room, I could watch the fire spread across the faces of the thirty-some participants. Patricia's story ignited something.

That gathering ended – except these things never do. Within an hour of our departure from that tidy bungalow, we got this email from our ebullient Australian host, Peter:

After you left, not 30 minutes after, a man came asking for help at our front property line. His name was Victor, and he wouldn't enter the yard. He was dressed cleanly in shorts and a collared shirt, and was very apologetic for bothering us, but asked if we could help him in any way.

He said he had just arrived in town that morning after traveling all night; that he had lain down by the water under a tree, and fell asleep. He had all his belongings and wallet with him in a bag. It was stolen while he slept. He'd already been to the Salvation Army and they told him that help would not be available until Monday (this being Saturday). He spoke to the police – and since he was a homeless Black man, they no doubt had some degree of suspicion.

I asked if he had somewhere to stay, and he said he didn't mind sleeping outside. His real concern was getting by until Monday with no money, knowing no one.

Now I had to laugh a little sarcastically at the ancestors, for this was outrageously obvious – in no way subtle – an opportunity for me to live what I got from the gathering. I had a flash of both Inette and 'Iokepa in that camping park and a resounding "Ah Hah!" echoed through my head.

My reply to myself was: "Here it is – my chance to give what I got to another. Go for it Pete!"

Victor still wouldn't come into the yard, so I told him to wait, I'd be right back. I got a couple bottles of water, three T-shirts, and a pair of pants, and put them into a bag with a $50 bill. I handed it to him. He looked at the bill, obviously thinking, "a $10 bill...maybe $20..." He couldn't believe it was a fifty. He was prancing around the sidewalk, shaking his head, raising his arms to the sky, saying words like, "Oh my God!"

Do you get the picture? I suggested that he go out and make someone else as happy as he felt at that moment.

So your words and intentions, 'Iokepa and Inette, rippled through me and out into another. Maybe 'Iokepa's grandmothers could take a bow.

It seems that we don't need to be living without an income on a Hawaiian beach to feel our connection to one another. We don't need to be sleeping in tents or car seats and eating oranges that fall street-side from trees, to feel the bounty of the universe. Our opportunities are endless.

Patricia's story. Peter's story. Write your own. Receive well, with gratitude. Give well, with gratitude for the opportunity. It's just a single motion.

May 2009

Identity Claimed

There are whole categories of assumptions Americans make. One of them – especially post 9/11 – is this. All air travelers must carry government-issued identification.

For so many years now ʻIokepa Hanalei ʻĪmaikalani has traveled the length and breadth of the United States, by air and by car, without one. It has not been an oversight on his part; he didn't leave his state or federally-issued ID card at home in a drawer.

After his first ancestral visitation, ʻIokepa fully claimed his national identity – *kanaka maoli* – aboriginal citizen of the nation of Hawaiʻi. Following only his grandmothers' guidance and claiming his destiny fully, he was no longer willing to compromise the identity to which he was born.

Embracing his identity is not exactly the same as *renouncing* that which asserts alternative claim. However, it did require ʻIokepa, who represents and instructs his people, to no longer carry an identifying card or number that bolsters the American claim of dominion over his sovereign Hawaiian nation.

Alternatively, ʻIokepa created a simple photo ID card on a friend's computer and had it laminated. It has his name, address, height, weight, and birth date. It identifies him accurately as a member of the board of directors of a *Heiau* Foundation, a sacred, protected

Hawaiian site that certainly does not issue identification cards. It has neither an expiration date, nor any official seal.

Since 2001, the dutiful TSA security crew at the nation's airports has looked hard at 'Iokepa's whimsical photo ID and either waved him through or earnestly inquired, "What is this?" or "Do you have something else?" 'Iokepa has asserted: "I'm a sovereign Hawaiian" and "No, I don't have anything else." In every case – racial profiling be-damned – this brown-skinned, long-haired aboriginal has been waved through.

All of this is prologue to a story I want to share.

'Iokepa and I were at the Seattle airport two weeks ago, heading to New Orleans.

We stood in the security check line, prepared (as usual) to take our carry-on laptop computer out of its case, to empty the contents of our pockets, and to remove our shoes. 'Iokepa, in line just before me, handed off his ID.

The man in uniform stared hard and asked the usual two questions. He received the usual two answers. He froze in indecision.

'Iokepa and I smiled.

He summoned his supervisor. The supervisor, a respectful young man looking for a loophole, leafed through the TSA catalog of "approved indigenous peoples." (I'll bet you didn't know there was such a catalog.) Hawaiians, apparently, didn't make the cut. He sighed over his choices; clearly this sweet man wasn't up to strip-searching my husband.

Instead, he said: "Let's do it this way."

He took us both out of line. He led us to his station. He brought forth a clipboard with a printed form. He asked 'Iokepa to fill in his name, address, and signature. Then he phoned the nation's capital and instructed 'Iokepa to answer any questions he'd relay from official Washington.

He warned me: "Don't answer these questions for your loved one." We all laughed.

Question one: "Who else lives at this address?"

'Iokepa stared. "No one, it's a Post Office box."

"Whoops," said our interrogator, "Wrong question. Who shares this Post Office box?"

Answer: "My wife."

Question two: "What highway runs nearest to this address?"

'Iokepa stood stock still. He answered nothing at all for what seemed like a long lunch – but undoubtedly could have been counted in seconds. *I'm* thinking: "Ours is a tiny Island – we don't have 'highways.'" But I'm holding my tongue as I'd been instructed.

'Iokepa later told me: "I wasn't about to say *Rice* Street" – named by the American Calvinist missionaries and colonizing sugar cane barons after their own. Instead, he traced the road to its original name, and offered Washington, D.C. this: "Nāwiliwili – it means winds that blow in all directions."

Apparently, the Washington official was satisfied. The TSA supervisor was clearly relieved. 'Iokepa had been wholly consistent with his mission.

We boarded our flight. The multi-million-dollar American security industry was served.

March 2009

Part I

Free My Husband's Nation - Unleash Hawai'i

It's Thanksgiving Day; 'Iokepa is threatened with jail. The challenge of *Return Voyage*, always and only moved by ancestral guidance, intensifies.

In the long, deep, ubiquitous story of freedom denied, of national identity obliterated, of oppression institutionalized – there have been wars waged, anger and violence righteously uncorked against oppressors.

But there has always been another way: the brave, singular acts of civil disobedience of Mahatma Gandhi, who ripped India's freedom from the British stranglehold without fist or sword; the disobedience of Nelson Mandela, who freed his South African indigenous people with his hands and feet in chains. And, of course, Martin Luther King, Jr., who staged sit-ins – illegal acts of defiance – against the established laws of his land.

Each of these men disobeyed unconscionable laws; each was imprisoned as a result.

"I cannot recognize a law that enslaves my people." 'Iokepa Hanalei 'Īmaikalani echoes their example.

It has always seemed so small, the substance of the specific *disobedience*: a seat at a Woolworth luncheonette; a swim in the local pool. 'Iokepa's lapse from adherence to the law of the land appears no grander. The issue at hand is small; the significance of the freedom call is enormous.

For thirteen years, my husband has refused to carry any identification that ties him to the United States. His grandmothers instructed him: "You will claim identity only to your Hawaiian nation." He dropped his hard-earned, twenty-six-year-old, flawless commercial driving license into the trashcan at the Kaua'i airport. He tore up his social security card and never again used that number.

He is a Native Hawaiian – a descendant of a 13,000 year lineage that binds him to his aboriginal roots. His nation is *Lahui* – the authentic name of these Islands. It means nation, tribe, or people.

When you are a Native Hawaiian and your ancestral grandmothers (who died long before you were born) ask this of you, apparently you do not refuse.

. . .

'Iokepa met me, on my brief vacation to Kaua'i from Portland. I encountered a man (without a car) who walked a minimum of ten miles a day. Walking became his meditation. If necessary, he hitchhiked.

When my son and I joined lives with 'Iokepa, we brought with us my 1991 Toyota Camry. It was registered and insured in my name. I am not *kanaka maoli* and I do not pretend to be one. I carry an American driver's license.

As I've said, 'Iokepa and I lived in that car for ten years (several with my teenage son). It was our home. It held almost all of our worldly possessions. We camped in tents out of it, and we slept in it.

For every one of those years 'Iokepa drove that car, and he walked each of the Hawaiian Islands as well. When we left the Islands for the first *Return Voyage* speaking tour, we gave that Camry away (then 16 years old).

Between the first and second tours, we returned home to Kaua'i for only four months. We had no car.

Our dear friends, a magnanimous couple, whose respective occupations involve healing, had just bought themselves a new car and had long-planned to surprise 'Iokepa with their old one: a 1998 Subaru Legacy wagon. It had an active registration until the following September, 2009. We left the car and Island just after Christmas 2008.

. . .

When we returned in September, the car's registration and insurance had expired. Without a U.S. drivers license, it's impossible to buy car insurance. Without car insurance, it's impossible to register an automobile.

So, on November 10, when 'Iokepa was driving his unregistered, uninsured Subaru on the streets of Kaua'i – without a government-issued driver's license, he was stopped and ticketed (by the rare officer who didn't know him). From the moment he rolled down his window to address the ticketing officer, he *knew* that it was time to speak his words on behalf of his nation inside a courtroom.

On February 11, he will go to court; he will plead not guilty. 'Iokepa: though faced with fines he cannot pay and with jail he does not seek, calls this an opportunity to raise the consciousness and change the consensus.

He enters court, less to challenge American law than to defend his people's right to their cultural and spiritual identity. He enters court to try to press past the fence that separates spectator and accused, to speak of a culture that "welcomed every guest here with open arms, open hands, and open heart." He enters court less to oppose than to embrace.

Let there be no confusion. 'Iokepa admires and supports the United States and yearns to see it live the fullness of its potential. But his Hawaiian blood and DNA make a prior claim.

"American law is this wide." (He holds his hands inches apart.) "It takes care of a few. My culture is larger." (He spreads his arms wide.) "It takes responsibility for every soul and every part of creation.

"There remain laws that require that I carry identification with a nation that isn't my own; that ask me to obey laws that remove me from my cultural practices and my identity. I cannot."

He enters court: the living embodiment of God's plan for the *kanaka maoli* – the Native Hawaiians. He enters court asking nothing for himself, and everything for his people.

When my brother asked me: "What if he loses?" I answered for both of us. "He cannot lose."

By that I do not mean that he will not be jailed. I do not mean that I want my husband shackled – or that my husband wants that for himself. We are not masochists. We very much prefer sleeping curled together. We savor our freedom.

But when I met 'Iokepa those many years ago, he warned me: "This isn't about us." And it is not. This is about a captive land, an oppressed people – and *their* freedom.

This small act of civil disobedience is a clarion call from a mountaintop to every one of us. Nobel-Prize-winning author Toni Morrison once wrote: "The function of freedom is to free someone else."

I ask: Let your imagination be your guide; share this small act; retell this oldest of stories – the freedom of a people to live their own culture, steward their own land, and speak their own language to the ears of their Creator.

Allow the Native Hawaiian people to teach the rest of us what is meant by *Aloha.*

November 2009

Part II

Inside a United States Courthouse: A Native Hawaiian Speaks

The Setting

The very first American Court House erected on the Island of Kaua'i was built in 1840, with complete awareness and intention on the top of the bulldozed ruins of what was the oldest *heiau* on this Island.

Heiau were (and those that remain are) sacred stone enclosures for Native Hawaiian ritual and spiritual practice, prayer and ceremony. Every heiau was built in alignment with the planets and the stars – with an ancient people's sophisticated awareness of the night sky. Each heiau sat within full view of the ocean horizon.

These sacred stone walls, built without mortar and standing tough for thousands of years, were deliberately destroyed to make way for an American claim on another nation.

After Calvinist missionaries built on the oldest heiau, they created and enforced laws that for almost 150 years denied Native Hawaiians: the right to speak their language in public; the right to name their children a Hawaiian first name (it had to be Christian); the right to use herbs and plants for healing; and the right to dance the authentic *hula*, which was prayer (never entertainment).

Only since 1972 may Native Hawaiians legally speak and name, plant and heal, dance and pray. They may do these things – but they no longer can. Cannot, because of colonial dishonoring and outright destruction of heiau, fishing beds, forests, land, and ocean; because of a two-century gap in genealogically transmitted knowledge; and because they have been shamed.

The imposed government outgrew their first Court House many times over. In August 2005, the county of Kaua'i dedicated a new and extravagant $42 million "Judiciary Complex," housing the United States courtrooms and the jail.

Now when you arrive by airplane on this lush tropical Island and leave the lovely, open-air, welcoming airport, you encounter first, this bulwark of the American judicial system. Before you see the inescapable ocean, mountains, or banana trees, you see this out-of-scale Judiciary Complex.

'Iokepa Hanalei 'Īmaikalani says succinctly of the huge investment of much-needed public money: "For some people, this building is reassuring – it makes them feel safe. For others, it's the death of a culture."

Thursday, February 10, 2010. 10:00 a.m.

It was to this building that 'Iokepa drove the 1998 Subaru from the Northwest edge of the Island to its center, an hour drive, with no driver's license. It was in the doorway of this building that 'Iokepa and I passed through security gates, temporarily relinquishing my purse and his belt, and made our way to the District Court for 'Iokepa's trial.

Oh, there were warnings aplenty, from sidewalk lawyers and real ones. His was an argument, they said, that could not be made in an American courtroom. There could be no precedent.

But it was an argument that innumerable friends and supporters prayed would be heard. Dozens of phone messages filled our usually quiet cell phone in the 24 hours before the trial. Dozens of emails filled the *Return Voyage* box. They sounded much the same: "Tell me the hour of the trial – I will be with you." Truly we felt that safety net of affection and faith.

For his "crime," 'Iokepa faced thirty days in jail, several thousand dollars in fines, and abundant court fees. We'd had, of course, no predictable source of income for thirteen years – our total worth on the day of the trial was twenty-four dollars and pocket change.

There were seven trials on the court docket this day. 'Iokepa's case was called fourth. He followed a child mauled by a dog, and a kid who had skipped out on his first court date. I don't remember the third. Each was represented by an attorney.

When his turn came, 'Iokepa walked through the gate that separated the spectator from the accused. He stood with his back to the seats behind; his shoulders squared; his mid-back-length silver hair shining under the fluorescent lights; his light brown eyes riveted on the judge. He articulated his full name clearly

– because even in Hawai'i (especially in Hawai'i) Hawaiian names are most often mispronounced.

The judge, a middle aged woman asked crisply, "Do you have an attorney?"

'Iokepa answered clearly, "I do not."

The judge said, "You should!"

He answered, "I won't need one."

"Do you want to hear the maximum punishment?"

"I'd rather hear the minimum."

He explained. "I'm not an American; I'm a Hawaiian, in my culture, with my people, on my Island. There is law, and there is justice. I'm asking for justice."

She responded, "I want you and the prosecuting attorney to spend a few minutes together outside the courtroom and see if you can work this out. "

The courtroom sat in absolute silence and waited. The judge appeared to read documents submitted to the court including 'Iokepa's written description of our life and service. She checked her watch repeatedly. I smiled to myself, absolutely certain that 'Iokepa's words were filling those conference minutes. After a half an hour, the judge asked the court officer to bring the two men back.

'Iokepa spoke his last words quietly to the prosecuting attorney in the doorway to the courtroom. I barely overheard him. He said "I know that you'll do the right thing."

It's a funny thing about those words that I've heard 'Iokepa speak before – even to a K-Mart manager about a defective, past-warranty beach chair. He says: "Those words make a person responsible."

From those words spoken in the doorway, to the table twenty-five feet away, the young prosecuting attorney, with shaking voice, recommended that the judge drop all charges other than the absent driver's license – and for that offense, he asked only twenty-one hours of community service, plus court fees – no jail, no fine.

The judge invited 'Iokepa to speak.

He began to describe our lives and its purpose.

"For thirteen years my wife and I have lived what the prosecuting attorney requires. Our life *is* 'community service' and that won't change regardless of what this court decides."

The judge shook her head in the affirmative. "Yes, I believe that's everybody's duty; I walk the beaches and pick up trash."

'Iokepa answered her. "Picking up *opala* – trash – is a good thing and necessary. But when I speak of community service, it's this. My wife and I lived in tents in the public parks for ten years among alcoholics and drug dealers, spousal and child abuse – the results of oppression. We did not get out of the tent and lecture people – we *live* so as to offer an alternative. I don't smoke, I don't drink, and I don't use profane language.

"I've stood in the middle of two men about to fight, and I've reminded them that this is not how their ancestors would have handled it. And you know, these men no longer fight, no longer drink.

"I call this 'community service.' I've never taken a paycheck. That is the culture I represent, taking responsibility for all people in all circumstances. This is our walk of faith. And it will continue whatever happens here today."

'Iokepa told the judge, "I didn't walk in here alone. My ancestors are here, and *your* ancestors are here."

The judge grinned.

'Iokepa considered the prosecuting attorney's recommendation for punishment and he said, "I don't think that I can do better."

The judge disagreed. She prodded 'Iokepa to continue the trial, call up the police witness who'd issued the ticket. "Because the prosecutor might miss something and then I can dismiss this case."

'Iokepa declined the offer.

In the end, the judge (who looked a great deal like the new U.S. Supreme Court Justice Sonia Sotomayor) said, "Thank you. I wish there were more people who felt like you do. I appreciate your statement. I apologize...I don't have a way to do more..."

And then the court clerk picked up the ball and reminded the judge that the mandated minimum $77 court fees could be reduced in this case for some legal reason. The judge laughed, looked at 'Iokepa, and said: "We just saved you $40 – the court fees will be $37."

'Iokepa answered: "Give that to me in cash, and we can all go to lunch."

Not one soul in that courtroom suggested or implied that he should get a drivers license or discontinue driving until he had one. Not one, not once.

It was obvious that the courtroom had been won over – judge, clerk, bailiff, prosecuting attorney, and spectators – all paying deep attention, all smiles afterwards. 'Iokepa had touched them. But he saw it differently: "It was the grandmothers."

Afterward 'Iokepa said, "I felt shot out of a rocket...the adrenaline. It was like the song you've never sung before, but you know the words. I felt that building *needed* something from the ancestors."

Afterward

Afterward, a dear friend who'd warned us of the impossibility of 'Iokepa entering the lion's den and exiting unscathed, expressed his awe: "You entered their turf – a U.S. courtroom – on your terms."

My husband and I sometimes disagree – vigorously. For the past three months, I awaited with extreme anxiety the results of this trial: none of which I could foresee would be to our advantage. My anxiety deeply annoyed and distracted 'Iokepa, whose faith in the protection of his ancestors is bullet-proof. One week before the trial, I surrendered that anxiety. I agreed that, whatever the outcome, it would be purposeful.

After a full three months of anticipation, I am struggling to let Thursday's events sink in. Hence my uncertainty, still, about which are the essential words among so many to be reported here.

'Iokepa, on the other hand, is nothing but excited to be used, as the court intimated, in those 21 hours – speaking to and for those most in need of his words.

In truth, for both 'Iokepa and for me, this small victory for human decency is just that – small. The morning after, he awakened and reminded me, "We have a prophecy to fulfill, and it speaks to freedom and responsibility – for all people."

I could say more, but I won't.

February 2010

The Story of Our Borders Bookstore:
It Is the Story of Hawai'i

The Story of Our Borders Bookstore

There was a time on our Island, not very long ago, when there were independently owned bookstores. But maybe thirteen years ago, the chain store Borders set up shop in the dead center of the Island. One by one the independents dropped off the map. It is pretty near impossible for an independently owned small store to compete with the mega-store and its deep discounts.

But our Borders was welcomed heartily and supported enthusiastically for so many reasons. *Our* Borders did not look or act like the corporate giant's other stores. It had a distinctly local feel, and the local folk were loyal.

It provided the only place on the Island where you could get foreign and national newspapers. It promised a book order would be fulfilled in one week – or the book was yours for free. It was home to the only coffee shop on the Island. And this coffee shop in no way resembled corporate Starbucks. It served salads picked from organic gardens across the Island and desserts prepared in local kitchens. It was staffed by some of the most dedicated and delightful servers I've seen in any coffee shop. The chairs and tables were clustered close to one another, and on an Island with a population of 40,000 then, 65,000 now, it truly became what it claimed to be: the Island's *Gathering Spot*. No conversation was private – all conversations were communal.

It was the place where you'd carry a birthday cake, call some friends, order some coffee, and celebrate. It was the place where young nursing students from the community college would cram together for exams – and someone else would step up to help. It was the place where you were most likely to find 'Iokepa and me during our ten "house-less" years. Some called it our "office." Many thought I worked there.

I knew every shelf in that place and almost every book. When a tourist made a request that confused a bookseller, I'd jump up and find the book. When friends gathered, we'd grab books from random shelves and discuss them, recommend them, and ultimately sell them.

You did not have to be either a book reader or a music aficionado to frequent our Borders Cafe. It remained the only place on the Island that collected socially, economically, politically, and ethnically disparate folks in a small congenial space.

It was the place you gravitated to when the heat was strong and the trade winds were not blowing for a cold drink and air conditioning; when the rains were chilling – for a warm chai or espresso. It was, inside and out (tables overlooking a magnificent green mountain), *the* place after a movie, a day at the beach, or a return flight from the U.S. It was the heart of community.

It was also the most profitable coffee shop in the entire Borders chain. The bookstore was beating itself in sales every single year.

And then, "Seven years ago it began to change," said the efficient and genial general manager for every one of those years. This was a woman who remembered and acknowledged every regular customer's name, health issues, and even vacation plans.

Corporate decreed: the newspapers from around the world were unprofitable. They were removed. Corporate decreed: you must stand in line again for a coffee refill – no longer trusted to fill your own. Corporate decreed: too many teenagers hung around the outdoor tables – remove the tables. Corporate decreed: local greens in the salad and fresh-made sandwiches were too expensive. Prepackaged, frozen foods were substituted. Corporate said: the comfortable reading chairs throughout the store encouraged readers, not buyers. The comfy chairs were removed. Special-order books now had to be paid for in advance, took three weeks to arrive, and too bad if it took longer.

Then: a few years ago corporate issued the coup de grace. The store would be enlarged and made to look exactly like every other Borders bookstore on the planet. The general manager's objections were ignored.

During the year-long renovation, the store remained open – but there was no coffee shop.

In that year the Borders habit was broken. When the store was unveiled one year later, it was huge, unfamiliar, and generic, with fewer books, more greeting cards, and many more useless gift items. There was a Starbucks next door to our Borders. *Our* Borders was no more.

The Island folks abandoned that made-to-formula store. The emptiness on most days and nights was eerie. The Starbucks tables and chairs were well-spaced; there was no longer a cross-fertilization of conversation or personal lives. *Community* had been successfully demolished.

It Is the Story of Hawai'i

It was 'Iokepa, who – when we returned home a few weeks ago to present *Grandmothers Whisper* at our local bookstore, and I found myself pressing my nose against the empty window of what used to be *our* Borders (now corporately defunct) – made the comparison that is the title of this story.

Three thousand miles from any large land mass, the Hawaiian Islands were the most isolated archipelago on the planet. The Native Hawaiians' connection to their Creator was direct and unimpeded. Their connection to every manifestation of their Creator's creation was compassionate, respectful, and intimate. For more than 12,000 years they lived in a culture without judgment, without greed, without ownership. Land, ocean, and sky were gifts of the Creator; impossible to claim; they belonged to everyone and to no one. Yet everyone was responsible. The Native Hawaiians *knew* something about the threads that make up the tapestry that is community – and they honored it. They had no war.

Their matriarchal culture was illuminated within the word *aloha.* At the heart of aloha is the word 'ohana. It meant: everything that you can see that you can wrap your heart around is your responsibility to take care of. It spoke of connections much larger than family.

But then a greedier, more aggressive people arrived, with colonial (corporate) aspirations (not unlike the chain store Borders), and imposed their foreign ideals and their greater-god, *individuality*. They brought hierarchy to these benign, egalitarian Islands – inflicted a nobility and a slave class. They brought to these powerful women and their respectful men, gender separation and racism, competition and fear. They brought war to a people who had refused violence in any form for more than 12,000 years.

The war they waged was against the soul of the native people. Then they re-wrote the Native Hawaiian story to suit their colonial appetites and to further their material ambitions – and they dared to call it "history."

'Iokepa says: "Borders came; they put everybody else out of business; they broke up the community – and then they went home.

"The same thing happened to my Islands and to my people. They came. They changed our identity. They demolished community. They went home."

The work of 'Iokepa's life (and his people's) is to reclaim and restore their indigenous identity and their empowering community, as a much-needed instruction to the rest of our bitter and suffering planet. He asks only for awareness – and prayer.

August 2011

Stealing From the Native Hawaiians Again: The Akaka Bill in Congress

The Bill

At the end of almost every *Return Voyage* gathering in these past years, well-intentioned folks have asked 'Iokepa: "What can I do to help?"

He answers: "When you hear that things are changing on the Hawaiian Islands – and you will – I ask that you offer a prayer for the Hawaiian people."

There is pending now, before the United States Congress, a legislative bill, officially named The Native Hawaiian Government Reorganization Act of 2009 – more commonly referred to as the *Akaka Bill*. Supporters across the United States have written us: "Finally, the Native Hawaiians will be recognized as the unique people they are – the theft of your land will be made right."

To our many friends, allow me to clear the political fog. The Akaka Bill – which has been bouncing around Congress since 2000, and which passed the House of Representatives a number of times, but repeatedly died on the floor of the Senate – is absolutely not the change 'Iokepa Hanalei 'Īmaikalani has in mind. Instead of freeing his sorely oppressed Native Hawaiians, this Akaka Bill slams the final nail into the coffin that has incarcerated the *kanaka maoli* since the arrival of the first Calvinist missionaries.

The intention of the Akaka Bill is to silence 'Iokepa and his brethren. The bill essentially says: "We (the government that was imposed at gunpoint) tell you (the native people who've inhabited these islands for 13,000 years) what you deserve." This Congressional bill codifies the existing reality: Accept what we offer and shut up.

The Background

Under this bill, all authority remains with the original colonizers, who were, when they first arrived, Calvinist missionaries, then their sugar cane baron sons, and then when sugar cane ceased being profitable, their real estate developing grandchildren.

Under the Akaka Bill, the transfer of 'Iokepa's nation into the hands of the U.S. Interior Department insures the federal government's continuing privilege. Those in power – either corporate or governmental – retain power. Those disempowered (the impoverished Native Hawaiians) remain powerless.

These aboriginal people, who have for 13,000 years welcomed guests to their Islands with open hearts, are asked now to relinquish their claim to freedom. Under the Akaka bill, they consent to become another Indian tribe, minus tribal rights to pursue land claims in the courts. It essentially legitimizes the land theft.

Still today, the grandsons and great-granddaughters of the two-dozen families who overthrew the Hawaiian nation proudly and publicly display a framed photograph on the walls of their homes. The photo cements their claim to Island "aristocracy." It captures the moment that their sugar cane cultivating ancestors held guns to the head of the last remaining Hawaiian monarch.

Queen Liliuokalani, gun to head, bravely held fast to her cultural values. In her final *aloha* she refused to shed her people's blood, and she was imprisoned by the men who claimed her land. The U.S. Congress rubber-stamped the take-over of this sovereign nation.

The perpetrators made their fortunes desecrating the land that fed a native people and outlawed every Hawaiian spiritual practice.

In 1993 (on the 100th anniversary of the take-over), President Bill Clinton signed a Congressional Apology Resolution, acknowledging the facts I've described and supporting the native claim. At the conclusion of the signing, Senator Slade Gorton (R-Washington) said in the Congressional Record: "...the logical consequence of this resolution would be independence."

'Iokepa's people have profound spiritual gifts that can and will inform the Earth's behavior. They are in no way or manner a political people – and that fact has been used as a knife against them. It has been in the political arena, for almost 200 years now that the gentle, loving, beautiful Native Hawaiian people have been disenfranchised in the name of greed.

The Confusion

The Akaka Bill is *not* what 'Iokepa or his people choose.

Native Hawaiian, Wesleyan University anthropologist J. Kehaulani Kauanui wrote in her recent book, *Hawaiian Blood*:

> But the paradox for the Kanaka Maoli is that the state of Hawai'i, and arguably the U.S. government, has its own investment in seeing this political goal (the Akaka Bill) obtained because it would limit Hawaiians' full sovereignty claim and extinguish land title – namely the kingdom, crown, and government lands – and thus settle the state's ongoing "Hawaiian problem."
>
> So...the federally driven legislation threatens to amount to yet another land grab in the guise of "Protecting Hawaiians."

Politics makes strange bedfellows. It is sometimes hard to tell your friends from your foes.

Passage of the Akaka Bill by the U.S. Senate, to date, has been withheld *not* by the Native Hawaiians themselves – who remain, as usual, rather powerless in this political conversation. It has been killed by the far-right. It has been killed by U.S. senators who argue, ironically, that any acknowledgment of a native claim to their culturally unique identity is "racism." In other words, the very people who brought the concept of racism to this isolated Island chain (where Native Hawaiians accepted all without judgment) are the same people now calling the kanaka maoli "racist" for claiming their cultural inheritance.

And the confusion gets thicker. The Office of Hawaiian Affairs, which is a state government agency that has been assigned (by the governmental and corporate powers-that-be) the role of "speaking for the Native Hawaiians" has spent millions lobbying on behalf of passage of the Akaka Bill – which would guarantee these political office-holders continued political influence.

No wonder our good friends are confused. No wonder the media is confused. No wonder President Barack Obama is confused. Each absolutely believes that this legislation might bring some healing to an indigenous people who die younger, live sicker, and are most likely to be homeless, impoverished, incarcerated. These are all well-meaning allies of my husband's people who have been victimized (and baffled) by the millions spent to pass this bill, the public relations blitz, and the rhetoric of fear. ("Without Akaka, you'll lose what little you have.")

In sum: The Native Hawaiian Government Reorganization Act of 2009 is a case of false advertising. It is not the ticket for good – unless by that we mean, "The missionaries came to do good, and they did *well* instead."

The Native Hawaiian people deserve to decide their own future. That cannot happen within the U.S. Department of Interior. The Native Hawaiians are *not* a tribe. They are a nation – and their nation is occupied.

April 2010

Welcome Home *Kanaka Maoli...?*

There are two distinctly competing versions of this story. Both are equally true. In *both* stories, 'Iokepa Hanalei 'Īmaikalani and I have just returned home to Kaua'i – the northwestern-most Island in the Hawaiian archipelago – after more than a year on the American continent. In both versions we loved touring the U.S. with our new book and in both versions we were yearning for home.

In the first version: last Thursday, we put up our great-in-the-rain-and-cold, but less-great-in-the-tropical-heat donated German tent. It is our fourteenth tent in thirteen years without a house on the beaches of Hawai'i.

In the first version of this "welcome home" story, we are swimming each morning in the cool, clear Pacific Ocean, removing a year of exhaustion. We are sleeping under the most incredibly vibrant canopy of stars – the Milky Way a visible blanket in the sky, the Southern Cross at the horizon. We are witnessing daily rainbows, dazzling sunsets, and walks around the Salt Pans where my husband's people have traditionally harvested the salt for thousands of years.

Equally gratifying on this return home: with every single step we've taken on this Island populated by 65,000, we are greeted by familiar and less familiar faces who have missed us and who let us know this in no uncertain terms. We are hugged by all, and by Native Hawaiian kindred we exchange breaths as greeting – in Costco, in Safeway, in the parks, on the beaches, at the Post Office.

We are welcomed by folks who have heard about *Grandmothers Whisper*, have looked at our website, but have waited until we returned home to buy their copy of the book. They (in the way of small places everywhere) wanted to get it from our hands with our stories. They wanted it *personal*.

Hawai'i is nothing if not personal. And that which is personal includes parts of creation that are not strictly speaking persons: the sharks, whales, sea turtles, albatross; *ki* leaf and *kalo* plants; coconut, mango, and banana trees.

So, in the first version of this story, we are welcomed home to a fairy tale: tropical beauty, people of good heart and compassion.

But I've never been in the business of writing fairy tales, so there is a necessary second version of this story. In this one my *kanaka maoli* husband (and I, by association) are made to feel much less welcome.

In this version, I sit next to my silent husband in the Honolulu airport on our way to Kaua'i and I say from my heart: "I'm sorry." And my Native Hawaiian husband – this man who has surrendered his life to the resurrection of his battered culture, people, and land – smiles slightly through an almost impassive mask, because he knows that I've read his heart. After so many years together, I can hear with his ears, see with his eyes, and feel with his heart.

I am *sorry* for so many things large and small which are in our faces from the moment we put out feet on my husband's sacred *ka 'āina*. I am sorry for the glaringly sunburned tourist who is making a joke of something she doesn't understand; she is mocking a *hula* that she has no idea was always and only prayer. I am sorry, too, for the man in the plaid Bermuda shorts who is describing in gruesome detail the traditional Native Hawaiian foods he found inedible at a festive *lū'au*. I am sorry that none of these innocent tourists feels compelled to consider the presence of a Native Hawaiian in their midst – and how their words and actions might sound to his ears. Or maybe they're not so innocent and they simply do not care.

I am sorry for the recorded announcement bellowing at the entrance of the airport on Kaua'i: "*Aloha*. Curbside parking is for loading and unloading only. Vehicles in violation will be ticketed and towed...*Mahalo*." I feel 'Iokepa cringe at the misuse of his beautiful Hawaiian language – *aloha,* in the presence of all of God's creation; *mahalo,* gratitude to that Creator – used to frame a TSA security threat.

'Iokepa murmurs quietly. "Because this is a state, they think they're entitled."

I am sorry that *only* in the Honolulu airport is my husband's refusal to carry state or government identification a cause of nastiness. In all our years of travel, his simple explanation: "I'm a sovereign Hawaiian" and a computer generated, laminated photo ID sufficed; we were always treated with respect. This time, on our last leg home to Kaua'i, a TSA employee (not, of course, a Native Hawaiian) shook his head in disgust and simply refused to engage 'Iokepa at all. This, only in Hawai'i.

And finally this:

'Iokepa and I have lived in tents on the campgrounds of Hawai'i for all of these years together. Each time that we have returned home, after swapping our "speaking-in-public-clothes" for swimsuits, shorts, and flip-flops, we set up our tent in the county beach park where we lived for ten solid years – the Salt Pans.

This time it went like this. We enter the familiar County Parks and Recreation office, looking for a camping permit. As usual, the person behind the desk asks our names, hits his computer button, and there we are: in the system for these many years. FYI: This permitting process is not about security, only about residency. Visitors are required to pay; residents are not.

But this time – to this sullen and taciturn man – our being in the system for more than thirteen years did not prove residency. Carrying a Native Hawaiian name and face did not prove residency. He wanted an ID. 'Iokepa handed over his laminated, computer-generated card. "I'm a sovereign Hawaiian." The man found it inadequate. Like the man at the Honolulu airport, he shook his head, disgusted. Like the man at the airport, he wasn't Native Hawaiian.

Apparently, there were brand new rules – new requirements to prove that you were not a tourist. You were required to produce proof that you voted in the most recent general election (sovereign Hawaiians do not vote in U.S. elections) and a valid Hawai'i driver's license (sovereign Hawaiians do not carry government-issued identification).

Apparently there is an exception to the new rules – always there is an exception: "All active duty military personnel stationed in Hawai'i" are automatically considered residents. Native Hawaiians are not.

We were bounced to this man's boss. Here the story takes an even more ironic twist. This man's boss turns out to be the park ranger who had personally checked the permit hanging on our tent every single morning for thirteen years at the Salt Pans. He'd been promoted to the desk job while we were gone. This is a small Island; we know one another well.

That should have boded well for proof that 'Iokepa is a qualified resident. John, with a serious beard the length of all my years on the island, greeted us warmly; we exchanged family stories. Then this: "I'll issue you a permit for just one week. I'll have to send this to the county attorney's office for approval."

With that said: he xeroxed 'Iokepa's computer-generated photo ID card *and* his Costco membership card. (Don't ask – it had his picture!) Further irony: not one person asked *me* for identification. Maybe that is because in the matter of colonization – that is, of American entitlement – I look the part. I have nothing to prove – but my kanaka maoli husband is suspect.

And that is the story: version one; version two. Both equally true.

July 2011

Change We Choose *Not* To Believe In

We've been off Island long enough to see (without blinders) the changes.

After more than a full year away, it has felt important in these past months to explore our old haunts, to revisit the paths we've walked together for fourteen years, the beaches where we've sunned and surfed, and the mountain where we've slept to the accompaniment of bird song. So when there is sufficient money for gas, and leisure time too, we do just that. We revisit; we reminisce.

We live on an Island in the middle of the Pacific, where for 13,000 years the native people took exceptionally good care of every *malihini* (guest) who landed – by boat and now by plane – on their shores. The *kanaka maoli* consistently and unconditionally shared their Island paradise – and asked absolutely nothing in return.

Perhaps that was their mistake. Perhaps their requiring nothing – not respect for human, plant, or animal life on their isolated Islands – foretold the future. It has been a future where the guests got accustomed to receiving every gift one human could offer another – and offering neither gratitude nor respect in return. At the heart of this ancient culture is the word *kahiau*, which means "giving with no expectation of return." And *that* Hawaiian expectation was more than amply fulfilled.

Perhaps, on the other hand, these native people, now crushed under their guests' claims and disregard, have made no mistake at all. Maybe the mistake is ours – those of us who've come ashore. We, who have arrived seeking satisfaction of our every material need, and ignorant of the cost to the land, the ocean, and the people upon whose shoulders we build our claims.

Maybe these good people, who preceded our occupation by almost 13,000 years, suffer quietly so as to awaken something quiet inside our own hearts. Maybe they live their refusal to relinquish the one thing that marks them as different now – their utter generosity, their unwillingness to separate our interests from theirs – so as to remind us. Maybe it was, and is still, a part of some larger cosmic plan. But that does not mitigate the pain.

Too easy to speak historically: Captain Cook, the sailors, the Calvinist missionaries, the sugar cane and the pineapple tycoons – and leave it at that. That was then. But in truth, *then* is now. And now, as 'Iokepa and I drive and stroll our home Island, it looks like this.

I tell small stories to reveal larger ones.

'Iokepa and I took a very slow drive up the side of the mountain not so far from the ancient, sacred Hawaiian site where we met and later married. We crept in and out of small roads, observing the changes to the places where we've so often walked together: a huge spreading banyan tree – gone; a quiet untamed streambed – now traversed with a walking bridge; wilderness – now cultivation; fruit trees – now potted plants; and most apparently, where there had been untamed fields to stroll – suburban houses.

But we were revisiting; we were trying not to judge. For years we've watched the encroachment of the guests' culture. Only the specifics were new, not the general direction of the change. So we crept along at perhaps ten miles an hour, and when we approached a set of houses that we'd last seen in the process of being staked out, curiosity seized me. I am, by defining nature, curious. I am also, by nature, a landscaper. The now "back yards" had been steep and unstable river edge. I wondered aloud how they might have built there, so as to reclaim that which the stream appeared to own. How had they done this?

From naive impulse and unfettered curiosity – not another thing – I asked 'Iokepa to stop the car. I opened my door and told 'Iokepa I wanted to take a look at what they'd done, at how they'd done it.

'Iokepa Hanalei 'Īmaikalani is a brave and outspoken Native Hawaiian. But for almost 200 years his people – his family – have been told in no uncertain terms to know their place, to not *trespass* on their ancestral lands. He would think 100 times before he'd step on a stranger's grass. He, by nature, would not join me.

I am a sixty-five-year-old, well-groomed, well-dressed woman with dark hair that is lavishly threaded with white. I cannot imagine how and who might find me threatening to their safety and security. It was broad daylight – a warm, sunny Saturday afternoon. I walked the unfenced grass border between two homes, smiling in the direction of the house, more than willing for any conversation, but not wanting to impose on the family activity inside. I didn't expect my exploration to take a minute – the yards were not deep.

As I passed, a window flew open; a man's head thrust through; he shrieked: "What do you think you're doing?"

I answered: "I'm admiring your home, your landscaping. I used to walk these…"

Face in flames, he cut me off: "Well you can't now. This is private property!"

"I'm sorry," I said. "I didn't mean to frighten you, or offend you."

"This is private property! You can't walk here!"

And so I silently returned to the car parked at the curb. We continued at five or ten miles an hour down the street and around the corner, trying to reclaim our equilibrium. 'Iokepa said not one word until we returned from the dead end and reentered the offending street. The man from the window was lying in wait, and 'Iokepa said only: "I knew that he wasn't finished." 'Iokepa stopped the car; the forty-something man raced across the street and raged directly into 'Iokepa's driver's window: "We don't want you here!"

I opened my door, walked around to 'Iokepa's window, and said: "Excuse me, but it's me you want to address. My husband has done nothing."

Then, softly I said: "Let me introduce myself…" and I told this man my name, once again apologized if I'd offended him, and restated that I was admiring his home. At this point, his wild-haired wife and ten-year-old son charged across the narrow street and joined us. She bellowed: "I home school my children and I'm very protective!" I repeated: "I'm sorry if I've offended you."

"This is our neighborhood and we don't want you here!" her husband spat at us. I quietly inquired: "And who is 'we'...?" He answered: "The neighborhood watch." Sure enough, there was posted on this street that used to be the empty field where we'd strolled together: "Neighborhood watch..."

Alone again, 'Iokepa pondered: "They fear that I want what they have. When in truth they want what I have: freedom, identity, culture. They assume that what is mine is for taking – what is theirs is for keeping. They have nothing that I want. They think I'm going to take something that they have stolen; they are fearful because they feel guilty."

Together we recalled a quite different exploratory drive several years before. On that day, we entered as strangers a remote, fishing village on the Island of Hawai'i. It was populated heavily with Native Hawaiians. We recalled how the assessing stares of strangers melted into smiles and hugs, shared mangoes and conversation. We recalled this other way of being that was *only* inclusive.

And so I repeat: perhaps this indigenous people live their refusal to relinquish the one thing that makes them different from us now – their whole-hearted generosity, their unwillingness to separate their interests from ours – so as to remind us of what we have lost and continue to willingly lose every single day of our lives.

November 2011

Destiny Served

"It's not that we have a right to life, but rather we have a responsibility for life."

Several months ago, 'Iokepa and tall, imposing Tiokasin GhostHorse shared a conversation across the radio waves in New York City, on Tiokasin's First Voices: Indigenous Radio. This morning, after a particularly intimate and probing gathering, I am remembering the prominent Lakota's words.

I have often said of my commitment to 'Iokepa, his people, and the fulfillment of this 1,000-year-old Hawaiian prophecy, "I didn't choose this life, as I've chosen so many things in my life (my jobs, vacation spots, and presidential candidates). This life chose me."

Among Native Hawaiians, to claim destiny is not to relinquish responsibility; it is, on the contrary, to claim full responsibility for the life each of us agreed to at birth. Those destined to be fishermen (or women) fished. Those destined to work in the *kalo* fields grew food. Those born to cut timber off the mountain did. Those born to sit under the coconut tree each day and meditate, sat without judgment. Though a child's name (a gift of the ancestors) implied, in metaphor, his destiny, it was his or her life's work to imagine it, and then fulfill it.

We moderns should only be so lucky – a name to instruct us. Nevertheless, our task remains the same. 'Iokepa insists: Each of us "made promises" when we took on human life. Each of us was armed with particular gifts to support the fulfillment of these promises. Like the Hawaiian child who carried the key to his life's purpose locked in a set of words that were his name (a set of words that could have dozens of possible different meanings), it remains our life's work to imagine and then fulfill our destiny. No one can do it for us.

That question surfaced around the dinner table last night with a dozen attractive, successful strangers: physicist, psychologist, writer, mediator, massage therapist, musician and artist.

"F...k spiritual teachers!" a tall and spindly, very accomplished artist blurted out over our beet soup. Apparently she had spent some years bent at the knee to one. "Have you outgrown your need for a teacher?" I asked, as tactfully as I could manage.

"She outgrew her need for them the day she was born!" the psychologist, spoon in hand, leaped in to make the point.

From the moment I met 'Iokepa, he has consistently asserted: "I'm not a teacher."

I have heard him repeat, more regularly than we now accumulate miles on the odometer of our Camry: "I don't have your answers. They come in many ways. *Ask*...get quiet...and listen. You'll get used to feeling the answer."

There are 160 words for the wind in Hawaiian, 138 words for the rain. Each one is the answer to a prayer. The indigenous peoples came to recognize those subtle differences – their lives depended on it.

But not only do the answers arrive in the wind in our face, they also come from a book that falls off the shelf – or from the words we overhear in a random conversation. We get used to feeling the answers.

As 'Iokepa says, no one can dictate our direction; no one can speak for our unique destiny; no one can "respond to that responsibility" for us. We are born with the answers. Our noisy, demanding modern world can quash our *'ike hānau* – our birth knowledge – but it remains inscribed in our cellular structure. All manner of loving ancestors are present, to remind and support us in our task.

Then – when, from the quiet chambers of our deep knowing, we recognize (hear, see, smell, taste, or feel) what had been ours for the picking – we are compelled to say an unequivocal "Yes!" to it. That, too, is our responsibility.

And finally, 'Iokepa's people remind us, like the gentlest of mothers, to say "thank you" out loud. From their gratitude was born ritual.

February 2008

Destiny Defined

I have written about destiny. 'Iokepa has spoken of it. He calls it the promise we made when we took on life. Yet there is persistent bewilderment among moderns who have refused it.

Echoing the Hawaiian grandmothers, I have written: no one of us is born with the same destiny; we're gifted with individual and cultural gifts to help realize our specific promises.

I'm a writer, not a doctor, sculptor, computer programmer, pastry chef, or automobile mechanic.

I'm a deeply Jewish woman – so my cultural gifts are not my husband's. He sees with his Native Hawaiian eyes the whales on a distant horizon; I don't. He feels the changes in the ocean water when a shark is nearby; I do not. I'm from a scholarly tradition; he is not. We share our gifts with one another; we celebrate our differences; we don't judge one another where we fall short of the other's possibilities.

'Iokepa's promise – his destiny – lies within his name. His full name translates: "The best from heaven (who is God) has chosen him, to work, to bring the people together." His work for the past sixteen years – cultural immersion on the beaches of Hawai'i, and now sowing the seeds of what he discovered – is the fulfillment of his calling.

But there have been some people – Native Hawaiian and other – who have read our story and have challenged us. "I have problems with your returning to the traditional life of our people, and yet not partaking in the traditional methods of feeding yourselves. Why did you starve instead of fishing or instead of growing *kalo*?"

'Iokepa answers: "I am not all Hawaiians; I am one Hawaiian. I don't own every gift of every other Hawaiian – nor anyone else's destiny. Through community we share our gifts."

He says: "I've fished, but my destiny is not as a fisherman; I've helped tend and clean *ka 'āina* (the land), but I've been in these years without land to grow food. My destiny – my work – lies within the name that I carry, and my cultural gifts are those that support that work."

Modern Hawaiians are like other people, critical of one another, judgmental at times. 'Iokepa's work is to remind them (and us) of the ancestral intelligence that all of us carry in our DNA – an intelligence that refuses judgment, competition, hierarchy, gender segregation, and of course, war. 'Iokepa's work on the Islands is in the face of those infections from the modern Western world.

People in the United States often ask us: "How do the Native Hawaiians respond to 'Iokepa?"

The answer: Often with tears of gratitude. Often like this: "The words you speak are *exactly* the words that my grandfather spoke."

And sometimes with challenges: "Why did you starve? Why didn't you do what your ancestors would have done?"

'Iokepa responds: "Not every Native Hawaiian was a fisherman or a farmer – and community always took care of those who were not. Now it does not. Apparently Inette and I needed to live that, to be able to speak about it now."

This has been a tougher time for 'Iokepa and me to live what the aboriginal Hawaiians lived effortlessly for over 12,000 years. We work to turn that around.

February 2012

Loss

'Iokepa's mother died yesterday. The only way we know to honor that momentous passage is a reprieve from *doing* – a seizing of "still."

The *Return Voyage* has slowed to a crawl.

In our lives on Earth, it is absolutely required that we honor the pauses. That we stop in our tracks – permit, at times, what feels like a loss of momentum. Within our industrial world, there is an addiction to motion – and a consequent avoidance of *still*.

It feels unnatural and unrewarded in an activity-addicted life to stop, to do nothing, to stand motionless and breathe. But we hearken to another world, another time, another culture – and it holds instruction for each of us.

'Iokepa's mother, my mother-in-law – a slight woman with whom 'Iokepa shares not a single physical characteristic – was the rock solid foundation of her son's life. Not another person came close to that; not another one was needed. She attended every high school football game. Maybe she winced; perhaps she covered her eyes – but she attended. She supported his passions.

She was in the bleachers for every wrestling match. She never missed a motorcycle race. It wasn't easy to watch her only son flirt at harm's edge. But in her eyes, he could do no wrong.

My guess is that the best of our mothers convince each of their children that they are her favorite. I know that 'Iokepa never doubted it.

At the end of his dangerous youth, his mother handed over still another gift. She presented him with a beautifully wrapped box. Inside: her carefully detached and ironed apron strings. This woman knew how to hold on, and she knew how to let go. That was her good sense.

She was challenged again twelve years ago, when her successful son left her side to undertake his part in the ancient Hawaiian prophecy that required him to relinquish everything he worked for all his life. Relinquishing cars and homes and things material was comparatively easy. Walking away from his aging mother in Washington State to return to Hawai'i and fulfill his destiny was hard indeed. She kept track of the days, months, and ultimately years since that day in 1997 when he left her side to take his place among his people – in their service, and at the service of their Creator. She died, not coincidentally, we know, on the anniversary of his departure.

She was proud, and she never let him forget it. He was the apple of this woman's eye. She *listened* to him in a way that few parents are able to listen to their adult sons and daughters. He spoke honestly to her mind and he spoke gently to her heart – until the very end.

Now it will be 'Iokepa's turn to let go. And it won't come to him in a neatly gift-wrapped box. He'll have to dig deep into his soul to find the place she left for him. But he will find it, as his wise Native Hawaiian ancestors have found it – in the still, quiet breath.

The *Return Voyage* slows to allow just that.

February 2009

The Meaning of Hawaiian Sovereignty

'Iokepa and I read a *New York Times* editorial page column, and sucked in our collective breath. We were aghast that the editorial writer could have so completely missed the mark.

In *honor* of the 50th anniversary of Hawaiian statehood, the *Times* writer began: "The 50th state turns 50 on Friday, and the strange thing is how wildly and jubilantly the islands aren't celebrating." The writer explained the lack of celebration: "The reasons are sad but obvious... Tourism is in the tank."

Because the task of opening minds and hearts is something we take seriously, I am compelled to respond.

Thousands of Native Hawaiians (both on the Islands and within the United States) grieve the fact of statehood. Native Hawaiians were resoundingly outvoted by the *malihini* – guests – that they had welcomed to their homeland. Being born on the Hawaiian Islands does not make anyone *kanaka maoli* – nor does dying there. Newcomers remain guests of a people who celebrate their connection to every living being. Decisions made about the past, present, or future of their sovereign land belong to those who carry that ancestral genealogy.

The history books aren't ambiguous. The independent nation of Hawai'i was annexed in 1898 in direct violation of U.S. law. In that year, the American government forcibly turned my husband's independent nation into a U.S. Territory – and turned Queen Lili'uokalani into a prisoner and martyr for her people.

The U.S. government acted at the behest of a dozen American pineapple and sugar cane tycoons – for the purpose of padding their bank accounts. Hawaiian sovereignty was eradicated at gunpoint. Fully 95% of all living kanaka maoli petitioned their opposition to Washington. It fell on deaf ears. The petitions remain still in the U.S. National Archives.

My husband's people have not changed their minds. They have not benevolently acquiesced to the theft of their native homeland.

The *New York Times* editorial writer mentioned in passing: "Underneath is the unresolved pain of the Native Hawaiians, unhappy over long unsettled land claims and economic disadvantage."

'Iokepa and I take another deep breath. It has been fully 185 years since the missionaries' sons discovered wealth in sugar cane and fenced the kanaka maoli off their own land. That many years since missionary-imposed laws forbade native people their language and every cultural practice.

All injunctions remained on the state's law books – and enforced – until 1972. The native people continue to suffer excruciating losses. In all ways, they are an almost invisible minority – tucked away in marginal geographic and economic pockets of ill-health, acute poverty, and crime.

'Iokepa Hanalei 'Īmaikalani, says: "God gave the stewardship of the Islands to the kanaka maoli. But there are people who believe they need to own them. They destroy the land and the ocean; they level our sacred places – and then they go home. But we have no other place to go – this is our home."

These gifted and compassionate kanaka maoli have suffered every known indignity of oppression; it continues still. Yet 'Iokepa says with passion: "We have not been conquered – no more than Gandhi or Martin Luther King, Jr. was conquered by their assassins. We have not forgotten.'"

Perhaps the greatest violation was not the law that incarcerated and murdered the holders of the knowing, that closed down the ritual and prayer, and that refused these people their own names. The greatest violation, I believe, was silencing another people's story. The guests came, they shut down the native voices, and they wrote their own version of my husband's family's story. We are all – every one of us – the poorer for it.

Celebrate statehood? You must be kidding.

August 2009

The *Means* to Hawaiian Sovereignty

'Iokepa and I return to our Islands. But before we step off the airplane, we take ourselves to task. We remind ourselves that ends never justify means, and that our only hope of influence is by living example – our observable behavior.

For many months and even more car miles, we drove the American continental freeways. But we spoke out, always, on behalf of this place and these people.

We return now to swim in the ocean and eat our ration of mango, papaya, bananas, and coconut. We return to watch the sun set and the moon rise over the Pacific horizon; to star-gaze without intrusive city lights; to follow the ubiquitous rainbows – in sum, to drink from source. We come home to be quiet and to listen.

We return to listen, but the people of these Islands ask us to fill *them* (ears and hearts) with what transpired in our long absence. They yearn for accounts of how the aboriginal cultural message was received outside of Hawai'i. They count on 'Iokepa to be an instrument of change; they expect it. It is a weighty expectation. But it rests easily on 'Iokepa's shoulders; he hands it off to his ancestors. He is simply, he knows, the conduit for their words and wishes.

Since 1972, when the culturally repressive laws were wiped off the books, Native Hawaiians have pleaded and fought for their freedom. They've struggled, too, for the resurrection of their battered land. From the moment that they were un-gagged, they have spoken: softly – with *hula* hands, in their mellifluous language, and in prayer; loudly – through the political *Sovereignty Movement* to the World Court, the United Nations, and the U.S. Congress.

Opponents of freedom for the Native Hawaiians mock the Hawaiian Sovereignty Movement as, "hopelessly divided." Where 'Iokepa sees passion, they see rage. Where 'Iokepa sees excitement, they see threat. Where 'Iokepa enthuses: "When it all comes together...!" they labor to make sure that it never does. Land developers, hotel magnates, and politicians have a lot vested in keeping the Native Hawaiians hopeless.

For thirty-seven years, the strength of the political Sovereignty Movement, like the brilliant Hawaiian moon, has waxed and waned. Tortured recurrently with dashed hopes, deferred dreams, and disillusionment, there has risen a tidal wave of despair.

Anger, 'Iokepa reminds his people (and ours), is the antithesis of what his original culture was about – what it has to offer the world. 'Iokepa comes to the table with something else.

The existing Hawaiian Sovereignty Movement has failed in any significant numbers to win the hearts of its people. To a people who've seen their homeland stolen and trashed, their culture kidnapped and commercialized, the sovereignty groups ask that their people give something *more* to a political cause: sign up and trust us.

But 'Iokepa sees it through a different – an apolitical – lens: pure culture, pure spirit. He says: "We begin with the things we can agree on."

His people yearn for change and they welcome it. 'Iokepa brings something *to* them. He reminds them of what has been taken: their self-confidence, cultural validation, authentic heritage – and the absolute certainty that what they uniquely possess, the entire Earth has been waiting to hear.

For 12,300 years, the indigenous people of these Islands embraced a culture that refused the possibility of war. We work to awaken that ancient intelligence – ritual practices that dissipate anger, prevent violence, foster harmony, and share their profound implications for the 21st century.

This conversation does not require a passport.

September 2009

A Movie Tour

There is a radically different Island reality than the one that 'Iokepa lives to speak.

So, we are home. We take our beach chairs, our Willy's coconut oil, and our books to one of the innumerable white sand beaches on Kaua'i. We plan to refresh our bronze skin tones (mine is more conditional) and immerse ourselves in the warm Pacific Ocean.

On this beach visit, we watch three small buses pull up and park directly behind where we're perched on our canvas chairs. Several dozen tourists pour forth, stretch their bus-stiffened joints, and prepare for lunch on the beach. They are quiet and unobtrusive.

But bold signs scream from all sides of their buses: MOVIE TOUR! And regardless of an American economic recession that might affect tourism in Hawai'i, the MOVIE TOUR! buses remain full.

Surely, there is nothing intrinsically wrong with traveling 6,000 miles to the most isolated archipelago on the planet to experience the actual setting of a memorable Hollywood blockbuster film: *Tarzan*, or *Blue Hawai'i*, or *Jurassic Park*, or *Raiders of the Lost Ark*.

But when these folks in their insular buses traverse our Island from their four-star luxury hotels to the Hollywood locale of a glitzy, multi-million-dollar extravaganza – and then back again for cocktails – they may just be missing something important.

They come, these visitors, seven million strong every year. They come because the weather is consistent. They come because the beaches are unsullied, the ocean is translucent, and the stretch of sand is less crowded than Atlantic City or Miami Beach. But there are countless immaculate beaches, clear waters, and empty spots to spread a blanket, across the face of this Earth – and most of them are closer to home.

They imagine that they come for the differences. They tell themselves that Hawai'i is *exotic*: *hula* girls, and flower *lei*, and *lū'au*. But I disagree. The principal reason that seven million tourists flock to the tiny Hawaiian Islands every year is this: they are safe and familiar – in the same way that people search out Holiday Inns because "There will be no surprises." They come to Hawai'i requiring that they *not* be challenged by another culture.

Herein, naturally, lies the distinction between travel and tourism. Between searching for the truly foreign – which will startle, discomfort, confront our assumptions about ourselves – and a trip to Colonial Williamsburg.

Those who have, over the years, moved here to settle – in retirement or in pursuit of entrepreneurial profit off the tourist's vacation fund – often cooperate in this venture, insisting on gated communities and familiar garden landscaping. Hawai'i is selling tourists a replica of American suburbia that resembles nothing so much as the home they left behind.

Every authentic Native Hawaiian cultural bump is flattened. The landscape is depleted of indigenous species. Koa and sandalwood are replaced with cactus and eucalyptus, geraniums and impatiens. Dogs, cats, and Hummers are imported – and every single import annihilates that which thrived for thousands of years in the isolation of the mid-Pacific. Daily, the sea turtle eggs are smashed under four-wheel drive jeeps. The breeding whales are frightened off by U.S. naval sonar.

In their place: Wal-Mart, Home Depot, Hyatt, Marriott; golden arches and Starbucks.

The aboriginal Hawaiians remain the biggest obstacle to the romance of tourism – that pursuit of the familiar. It was essential, first of all, to remove these half-million natives from the land of their ancestors for development. It was necessary next to destroy their culture, because at the heart of their culture lay a core reverence for *ka 'āina* – their land – an awe for each element in creation.

So it turns out that Hawai'i can only be prepared for its *malihini* – guests – by the destruction of its hosts. When those guests arrive armed with cameras to capture the *exotic*, sunscreen to block the inevitable, and suitcases full of lives in other places, they can remain fairly confident. In their two-week stay, they will never see genuine hula. They will not hear the *kahiko* – that ancient mellifluous language spoken to the Creator's ears. And there is a better-than-average chance that they will not meet a single Native Hawaiian, who now lives in one of several pockets of poverty, ill health, early mortality, violence, and addiction.

Vast expanses of these native lands have been expunged of their natives – through imposition of foreign law, overt land theft, and taxation – and these natives have been resettled in tiny, dry ghettos of oppression that 'Iokepa calls "reservations." The Hawaiian State Department of Business, Economic Development, and Tourism labors overtime to make sure visitors never see them.

The seven million tourists who arrive each year implicitly agree to this arrangement. It's safer to climb onto the movie tour bus for the trip to Fantasy Island. The real Island just might spoil their vacation.

June 2009

An Unlikely Subject:
Hot Rods and Drag Races

The material and successful life that ʻIokepa Hanalei ʻĪmaikalani surrendered years ago, to take up arms and heart against the deception and suffering visited upon his people, included "Seven cars and a hot rod."

Despite the fact that his lavish passion in these past years has been solely cultural – language, history, and spiritual practice – for the first forty-six years of his life, he expended an equal dose of passion on cars that go *very* fast.

For fourteen years now the only fast-moving vehicles in ʻIokepa's life have been in his dreams. He awakens from sleep no less than twice a week behind the wheel of a race car.

He reminds himself and others: "You don't give away gifts that you don't value. The giving is the *giving* because you value it. I loved my life before…"

On the cusp of ʻIokepa's 61st birthday this year, he and I were traveling the American highways on book tour, telling our stories and disseminating the Hawaiian experience. Sometime in February, we were heading east on Interstate 40 out of Albuquerque, and the opposing lanes heading west were filled with multi-million-dollar rigs carrying the likes of the premiere NHRA racing teams and their incredible hot rods. The "season" was beginning the next weekend in Pomona, California. I could hear 'Iokepa salivate.

I am ignorant of this world that my husband occupied before we met, but I know my man, and I know the sound of his passions.

That night, in the stillness of a Louisiana motel room, I used Google to locate the NHRA (National Hot Rod Association) 2011 season race schedule. I looked simultaneously at the calendar for our book tour.

'Iokepa's 61st birthday was April 2.

The April 15 race weekend was in Charlotte, North Carolina. In the week before that we had scheduled a bookstore event in Roanoke, Virginia – a three-hour drive away. I realized: this *could* happen. I could offer 'Iokepa tickets to the Charlotte Speedway – to the drags for his birthday.

And so I did – and so we did.

In preparation we bought ear muffles. The sound of a well-running, nitro engine is music to my husband's ears – but deafening nevertheless at excruciating decibels.

On race day we patiently waited out tornado winds and torrential rains, visiting 'Iokepa's old chums in the pits where the drag cars are tweaked and tuned until they reach the staging area. We were surrounded by stereotype-defying crowds of every age, ethnicity, and socio-economic background.

The races were loud; they were brash. The sport challenged my learning curve. 'Iokepa's eyes sparkled, his blood pressure climbed, and he was awash with nostalgia.

So in the midst of this deadly serious occupation of ours – the grandmothers' whispered messages, and (as 'Iokepa often tells it) reclaiming a nation – we had a day of noise and un-muffled pleasure.

'Iokepa Hanalei 'Īmaikalani came home with a T-shirt.

April 2011

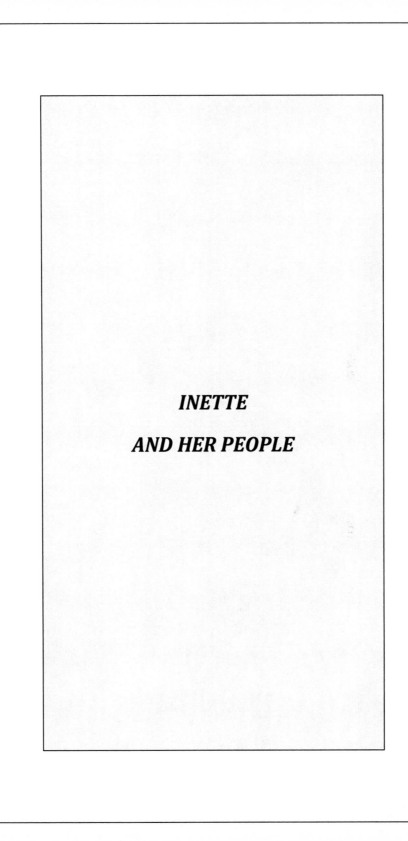

INETTE

AND HER PEOPLE

What's a Nice Jewish Girl...?

I realized, when Yiddish words began to creep unconsciously onto our website, that the time has come to declare myself front and center. To answer the implicit (and often explicit) question: Why is a decidedly Jewish woman speaking on behalf of the Native Hawaiian people?

Let me be very clear on this one. I met 'Iokepa Hanalei 'Īmaikalani on a vacation. I knew nothing about his aboriginal culture – I didn't know that there *was* one. I went to Hawai'i, as many do, for a respite from the stresses of a modern life. I went to Hawai'i to lie on the beach, get a tan, swim, and do almost nothing else.

Two days later I met 'Iokepa. Our souls met first. Our human forms took a bit more time. I fell deeply in love with the man. I felt the clear call of that elusive word, *destiny*. But I could not fathom how his work could possibly include an observant Jewish woman, an ambitious career writer from Baltimore.

After a couple of very challenging years into our merged lives, I still asked, and continued to be asked, *"Why me?"*

We've been together more than fifteen years now. Our speaking tours and the participants in every single gathering have shed light on that question.

'Iokepa is the Hawaiian. Only he speaks of the spirit of his culture, of the ancestors who guide and inspire his every move. I am the Jewish woman – deeply connected to another ancient culture. And because I am steeped in another wisdom tradition, I am able to understand much of what the *kanaka maoli* know and value.

At the most primal level, we share (and treasure sharing) the similarities: the essential faith; the divine connection that lies in our breath; the inviolability and power of the vibrations sent to the ears of God on our ancient languages. We share too a reverence for ancestral lineage, ritual, and tradition.

From the get-go, 'Iokepa (who was equally ignorant of my traditions when we met) insisted that I stay the path, live my culture, and observe my rituals. I have done just that. He has been at my side for *Yom Kippur*; I have been at his, at ancient *heiau*. We share the deepest respect for the antiquity and vitality of our spiritual traditions. We look for places where they meet – but we don't overstate them or pretend that we are who we are not.

In this lies an enormous power. We believe that the reach across the divide – that *could* separate strangers of decidedly different backgrounds – is where the divine on Earth resides.

I am a Jewish woman whose people have known thousands of years of oppression, and a fairly recent effort to exterminate every last one of us. I have said time and again in our gatherings, "If there is a single gift of sustained oppression, it is not the willingness to claim oneself as a victim. Rather, it's our simple refusal to countenance oppression in any form to *any* people."

So that's one gift of my Judaism. I see, with eyes that refuse to accept a lie, the degree to which 'Iokepa's people have been tyrannized by a colonizing culture. I see the poverty, the ill-health, the addictions, and the dysfunction that accompanies these almost two hundred years of oppression – and I refuse to ignore, romanticize, or contribute to the Hawai'i State Office of Tourism's fiction.

'Iokepa speaks uncomplainingly of the profundity within his ancient traditions; I speak about the pain of modern Hawai'i. 'Iokepa sings the praises of his enlightening ancestral heritage; I speak out about the true history that has been distorted by the missionary accounts.

When he speaks of the importance of the breath, the authentic language, the faith – I echo those traditions, and remind our gathering that he speaks for all of us. We are each descendants of indigenous cultures. There are gifts for every one of us to claim.

So 'Iokepa and I come together across that seeming insurmountable divide of culture and spirit. We solemnly aspire to live within our marriage and within our hearts an alternative to the cultural demand that we draw fixed borders around our differences, or even worse, that asks us to surrender the solemn gifts that define our differences.

There is a single personal consequence of these gatherings that take us from Bismarck to Baltimore. Open-minded and good-hearted men and women have continued to sanction the differences between 'Iokepa and me. Almost without exception, they have understood and affirmed the reasons we walk this life together. And after fifteen years, I no longer ask, *"Why me?"*

December 2012

Tsunami (*Kai eʻe*) on the Shores of Hawaiʻi

For every memorable year of my adult lifetime, I have had just one recurring and terrifying nightmare. In that dream, I am running for my life from a rapidly approaching, formidable wall of water that I cannot outrun. I am absolutely certain that it will overtake me.

Ironically, for every memorable year of my adult lifetime, in all of my many domestic and foreign homes, I have never lived anywhere near that possibility. I never once lived on the edge of an ocean – until I met ʻIokepa, and moved my life to these Hawaiian Islands.

I've never had that nightmare since.

This Saturday past, I was awakened at 6:00 a.m. – not by the usual annoying and pervasive wild roosters, but by an air raid siren. (I was dreaming, as it happens, of Bess Myerson, the first Jewish Miss America, chosen in 1945 at a time when her religion was a significant factor working against her selection.)

ʻIokepa also awakened to the sound of the sirens and said immediately, "Kai eʻe!" It means, in Hawaiian, "tidal wave." When you live on a speck of rock in the middle of the vast Pacific Ocean, hurricanes and tidal waves are part of your consciousness. They are not nightmares; they are facts of life.

We turned on our cell phone; we turned on our computer. Since three in the morning, our silenced phone messages had been screaming warnings from family on other Islands – various versions of "Get to high ground!" The rebooted computer shouted email alerts from friends across other time zones. We have spent much of our lives here living in tents on Kaua'i beaches. Friends and family feared for us.

But this time we were blessedly high and dry. It was our turn to offer help to our friends whose homes were coastal and in danger – people with farm animals in need of rescue, people in need of a place to escape.

Every hour from 6:00 a.m. until 11:00 a.m., with a final blast at 11:15, the sirens screeched their message of doom. Roads were closed. Helicopters circled remote areas looking for folks without phones or computers or radios; there were plenty.

We gathered with our neighbors on the highest ocean promontory near our home. It was hot and sunny. The distant ocean below our lookout seemed particularly flat and still. People brought food and picnicked. Hours passed, and the threat passed as well. The kai e'e missed the Island.

So for the first time in my life, I live in a place where tidal waves pose real and absolute disaster – and I no longer have that nightmare. Clearly, the terrifying wall of water that threatened me, that I could never hope to outrun, was something symbolic – a metaphoric fear that no longer needs to awaken me.

I suppose that once I'd given up my comfortable home in Portland to live in a windblown tent on tropical beaches... That once I'd agreed to enter the aboriginal nether-land between the solidity of my five resolute senses and the fuzzier world of ancestral spirits... That once I'd risked life, limb, and sanity to leap full-steam ahead into this improbable journey with 'Iokepa... Once I'd agreed to all of that, I suppose, I'd already lived through the tidal wave.

March 2010

The Power of Words

I've been a writer all my adult life (and much of my childhood). Words have consistently defined me. They are how I come to know what I think, and how I feel.

But words are important to a much larger audience than professional writers. "Language," cognitive philosophers have said, "is the mapping of a culture."

To know a people, we must know the actual meaning of their words. To know that meaning, it helps to be standing where they stood when they spoke those words.

So perhaps it is not surprising that when 'Iokepa is asked to recommend books about his people or his culture, he begins here: *The Hawaiian Dictionary* by Mary Kawena Pukui and Samuel Elbert. It's the definitive study of Hawaiian language, and it carefully distinguishes the authentic from the anglicized – the literal from the metaphoric.

We spent a titillating evening at the Poets House in New York City last Saturday night. These simple rooms in downtown Manhattan have served as the reading, writing, studying, and gathering place for three generations of America's most talented word enthusiasts. These rooms and its iconic library have helped define American literature.

On this particular night, the Spring Street address was packed with celebrity writers reading their poems aloud, eating and drinking among some 45,000 volumes of poetry, and commemorating the end of an era. Poets House was giving up its home.

Interestingly, the Hawaiian people spoke only in poetry. Their lyrical language sings with symbolism and metaphor. Translation from Hawaiian to English turns a simple sentence into a full paragraph. A Hawaiian paragraph takes an English page to explain.

I'm reminded of Chief Joseph Seattle saying: "It does not require many words to speak the truth." The Native Hawaiians would agree.

I say none of this to intimidate non-speakers. The overwhelming majority of indigenous Hawaiians no longer speak their native tongue. For almost 150 years, occupying missionaries and their sugar cane cultivating offspring mandated that the Hawaiian language not be spoken in public. For generations, Hawaiian parents forbade their children to speak the native language even at home, lest they slip in public and be shamed or punished.

Think about that. When we refuse a person his or her own language, we eliminate his ability to express not just his ideas, but his feelings as well.

For just a moment, imagine what that means.

November 2007

Politics as Usual

The place: Cleveland Heights, Ohio. The setting: a huge table topped with clams casino, prosciutto, Grandma Antoinette's incredible pasta sauce, a beautiful feta-topped salad, and champagne. The gathering: one old friend, and many strangers. They are scientists, medical researchers, writers, and accomplished artists. The time: one night after the Iowa presidential caucus. In sum: this was a group of serious intellectuals of a decidedly Democratic Party bent.

Wiry, intense Sally began the conversation with: "Is *Return Voyage* political?"

I answered, "There are elements of the Native Hawaiian experience that are political and there are sovereignty groups that address them. But *Return Voyage* is about finding common ground, identifying the cultural and spiritual strengths all humans share."

Sally turned, looked toward her other neighbor, and talked about Obama. She never looked back.

I confess to a distinct empathy with Sally. I'd been a political reporter and war correspondent for much of my early life and I continued to be a political junkie long after.

Naturally, in those years living on Hawaiian beaches with no predictable source of income, all money that found us was spent on food – never on that supreme indulgence, a Sunday *New York Times*. My addiction to news took a decided hit. But on that night in Cleveland Heights, with 'Iokepa to my right and the party (lively and loud) snaking a long table and busily dissecting the relative strengths of Obama, Clinton, or Edwards, I, like an alcoholic taking a single sip, felt that old zest returning.

I dove in. And yet the water felt quite different than it had before my immersion in Native Hawaiian culture. The political catch-phrases felt predictable and shallow – though clearly these people were anything but.

My husband, articulate and charismatic in any social gathering, sat silent, stoic as a Buddha. Silently, he was refusing to be drawn into what he called someone else's *reality*. He was insisting that we each define our own. His culture's reality was never political.

Finally, when the conversation turned to a very American political issue – Creationism versus Evolution – 'Iokepa entered the fray and the table made way. He simply refused that dichotomy. He insisted that other people's questions too often define our answers; that we must not allow it. Our choices are wider and deeper than the political pundits, the journalists, and the intellectuals allow.

The work of *Return Voyage* is not political. The Native Hawaiian people were not politicians. They were spiritual – deeply connected to the web of nature. 'Iokepa says, "They didn't see a category called *spiritual*; they just lived it. They knew their part in it – and they went out and shared it."

Perhaps the next time someone tells us that the solutions to the world's problems come only through our politicians and our political process, we might discover the strength, the imagination, and the insight to find a different answer rooted within ourselves.

January 2008

Mothers and Daughters – More or Less

For the past two weeks I've been blaming the heat. And yes, it's been a record-setting 100 degrees in inner-city Baltimore, with an unconscionable level of humidity. But yesterday I realized, that is not it – not my problem at all.

Allow me to explain. My oldest brother is a professional man. He was the apple of my father's eye. My next brother, the self-proclaimed "middle child," tried harder. He took over the family business and cared for our aging father every day of his life.

I am the third child – the only daughter. My father cherished me without reserve throughout my childhood and worried about me every day thereafter. He fretted over my every deviation from his feminine ideal and expectation.

When our father died after a brief illness some years ago my brothers' loss seemed inestimable. I grieved then, and I continue to cherish the memory of that honest and generous man. But what I've been living in these past weeks during this scorching Baltimore summer is something else entirely. My feelings now are far more complex.

My mother: inch by gradual inch I am losing my ninety-eight-year-old mother. It has not been the heat that has drained me. It has been the enervating emotion watching my familiar mother become much less familiar.

I am a woman. This is my *mother*. I stand in front of any mirror and I see her: in my curly hair, behind my smile. Sometimes it's a struggle to see where she ends and where I begin.

I have an iconic teenage memory. We are locked in a department store dressing room, waging warfare over some obscure matter of taste. We enlist the hired help (a saleswoman who foolishly dares to offer an opinion) to intercede and defeat the other in a staged battle over hemline length, ruffles, glitz, color, or neckline. We *define* our relationship for many years by the clothes we refuse to wear – and those we do.

I have an iconic adult memory. I'd been a vegetarian for nine years. My mother makes a thick chicken soup for me when I arrive alone for dinner. She insists, "But poultry is not meat." This is not an ignorant woman.

I remember, of course, my mother's vehement objection to *both* men I married. The first: "He's not Jewish." The second: "You hardly know him." I remember her caveat to my life as an author. "The only women writers who succeed have rich husbands who support them."

I could go on. I believe that almost every woman can – and does. The songs we sing with our mothers are seldom two-part harmony.

Regardless of the stories, the complaints, the engaging and the disengaging; regardless of the complexities of being the strong daughter of a strong mother – this is the parent who knew me then, who knows me now. This is the person who loved every bit of me (however much she objected). This is the woman who ultimately accepted (and found reason for pride) in my every choice – no matter how far I wandered, or how incomprehensible those choices were to her narrower life experience.

Today, I enter her apartment at the senior community (where she moved two years ago when we agreed that ninety-six might be a good age to stop driving) and her eyes laugh and dance. She tells me: "I love having you here. I love you very much!" Her entire petite body speaks that truth.

I am losing her. Not like my father after a three-month critical illness. My mother lives and breathes and walks, every day more slowly and with increasing fatigue. She remembers selectively and surprisingly. She forgets what she had for dinner, or whether she even had it. She no longer has a "yesterday" or even a "this morning." Time has disappeared. My mother teaches me still. She instructs me in the absolute value of this breath, *this* moment – gone!

This is a woman who has lived life with enthusiasm and zest from the moment she took it on. Mollie with the "million dollar smile" accepts life. She has systematically accepted difficult women among her many friends. She explained them like this: "That's just how she is."

She accepts, too, the losses. What has been acutely painful for me to witness, has been far less terrible for my mother to live.

Return Voyage alights here for three hot summer weeks. 'Iokepa and I are house-sitting our son's cats and plants in a downtown Baltimore neighborhood. Our son and his wife vacation in Cape Town, South Africa at the World Cup. We're here for my mother.

Mollie Speert Miller may live to be 105 – only God has that answer. Her health is perfect. But her body, her ninety-eight-year-old body – skin, bones, and brain – is simply wearing thin. I watch my adorable mother and I am helpless with grief. What she accepts, I continue to deny.

Mothers and daughters – there isn't a more fraught and complicated relationship. I cannot imagine a life without it.

June 2010

Not Every One of Us Is a Parent But...

...Every last one us is the son or daughter of a couple of them. So choose your perspective here. I can tell my story from the only perspective I have: the singular daughter of two very specific people; the mother of two very specific sons.

But like all writing, the micro or anecdotal only has meaning if it sheds light on the universal.

When I was a very unbending, recalcitrant young woman – rather sure that I was smart and even more certain that my parents were stupid – my mother would calmly say to me: "Wait until you have children." My mother was not wishing me a dose of that which I was dishing out; she was truly incapable of that. She was advising me that *then* I would understand.

In later years, when she would repeatedly refer to the degree to which I had caused her worry or trouble, I would genuinely draw a blank. I'd repeat over and again, "But I was such a *good* girl." I would silently list the possible directions I did not take: drugs, promiscuity, unwanted pregnancy, poor grades.

Apparently, none of that was what my mother had in mind. Inevitably, I did have children, long-delayed by my parents' expectations and standards. And frankly, I still didn't understand.

I gave birth; I reared infants, then toddlers; I rode out thirteen years of single motherhood to soccer games and bar mitzvah – and still I didn't understand. Still "trouble" did not compute.

But this week, my dark-eyed baby boy (the *easy* one in childhood) – somehow grown to twenty-eight, now lean and long – is offering me the dawning awareness of exactly what my mother had in mind. I am now on the ride of a lifetime – what my mother knew in her "stupidity." It was *then* (and it is now) the child who clung hardest to his mother's perfection – kicking, with everything he's got, to build distance.

It is mean-spirited, rude, and heartless in ways than any witness would attest to on a stack of bibles. Yet he sees himself (as I most certainly did back then) as faultless. He has graduated college with glowing recommendations from adoring professors who praise his willingness to help without recompense, his unselfish humility, his creativity, ingenuity, sheer intelligence, and promise. He put himself through college working minimum wage jobs in New York City; he graduated magna cum laude.

But *this* week alone, my son in a wonderful and rare visit during which we shared long walks and deep conversation about literature, told me, "You don't do anything," and in the next breath, "Your psychology is meaningless."

I suffered his refusal to share a thing with me one moment (icy silence and no eye contact) and to share his very heart in the next.

And after I'd made him a week's worth of his favorite breakfasts and dinners: "You can get your own glass of water." (He returned with only one for himself.)

I well recall a story that I'd heard many years ago about a tribal rite-of-passage somewhere in Africa. When the young boy was leaving the village with the men who would initiate him into manhood, there was a ritual. It went like this.

"Son," the mother asked, standing in her doorway, "would you bring me a cup of water?" Her dutiful son went to the spring, scooped the cup of water, returned to the doorway of his home – and threw the cup of water in his mother's face.

This week, my *easy* son did what he had to do. I wonder whether it took him this long to stir in me that awful pain of reaction – or has it taken *me* this long to realize that my mother's prognostication was on the money.

Mom, I finally understand.

March 2012

Hands in the Garden, Heart in *Ka ʻĀina*

I was born on Mothers' Day, the much valued daughter after two sons. Mothers' Day has always had a resonance to my little family.

It is a terribly long distance from the Hawaiian Island that ʻIokepa and I call home to the places where my sons and mother call home – six thousand miles to be exact. But this year, by happenstance, we landed in Baltimore (between a book signing in Rehoboth Beach, Delaware and a scheduled speech in New York City). I was able to share Mothers' Day across three generations with my ninety-nine-year-old mother and my thirty-year-old, first-born son.

Here is the gift that gave me prodigious joy. On Mothers' Day, my daughter-in-law Elizabeth and I browsed plant nurseries in search of the basics for her first flower garden. Her garden is confined to the tiny front and back yard of an inner city neighborhood. We took out our spades, our imaginations, and our fingers and caressed that tiny yard into a thriving bounty of blossom and color. I can't think of another activity that would have given me greater satisfaction.

Elizabeth is a most accomplished woman – a scientist at Johns Hopkins University who travels to Africa on her public health projects with the frequency that most of us attach to trips to the mall. Though her grandmother in Tennessee was, and is still, an adept gardener, my daughter-in-law never had the opportunity to plunge hands in the soil herself. She was determined to change that.

For most of my adult life, hands in the soil were the daily antidote to seven or eight hours constructing words on a page. It was the other half of my life – the part that took me from head to heart, from computer screen to dirt under my nails. It was how I unwound after the cerebral search for the right word, and searched instead for the right bulb in the right spot. I pulled my young sons along the garden edges: "Tell me the name." I'd remind them daily: "peonies...day lilies...rhododendron...azaleas, tulips, iris, daffodils."

But my years in Hawai'i have been what 'Iokepa prefers to call "house-less" in favor of the more pejorative "homeless." So I have lived upon the most fertile soil on Earth in a warm and tropical climate – and I have been, for the first time in my adult life, without a garden.

Within that paradox lies the story of the Native Hawaiian people, God's stewards of these isolated Islands. The *kanaka maoli* knew for a fact that land could not be the property of man, only his or her responsibility to care for.

But then their guests arrived – Americans and Europeans, who thought in terms quite alien to the Native Hawaiians, who thought in terms of *mine* and *yours*, who assumed responsibility primarily for turning fertile land into profit, and who, most of all, forgot to be grateful.

So I use this Mothers' Day opportunity to thank my daughter-in-law for the reminder: that little garden we worked together last Sunday was a gift to both of us. To thank, as well, my husband's people: they live to remind us that ka 'āina, the land, can be valued without being priced, can be lived with instead of upon, can be shared without being owned. All of this costs us no more than gratitude.

May 2011

Musing in Minnesota on American Medicine

It was a beautiful, crisp day on the North Shore of Minnesota. Our Swedish hosts led us up one hill and down again. We hiked through the thick white stuff on the ground, and through the flimsy flakes in the air. Because these were exemplary hosts, they had warned us well: "Watch your step; there are ice patches under the snow." We heeded them: up the hill, then down it again.

But within twenty feet of their front door, clutching a few Lake Superior stones in my left hand, I carelessly placed my booted foot – and the solid Earth slid out from under me. I fell hard on the open palm of my straight right arm.

The pain shot up the length of my arm; I couldn't get myself up. When I was helped to my feet, I started to black out. Our hosts offered the local hospital for an x-ray. But the price of health insurance was never factored into the life that 'Iokepa and I have led. Eating remained our priority. I demurred.

We spoke at a gathering the next night. I compensated with my left hand – turning doorknobs, using forks – awkward, but possible.

A week later, still unable to use my right arm, we were in Rochester, Minnesota for another gathering. Our host, a scholarly research nurse at the unrivaled Mayo Clinic, offered us a tour of her place of employment.

Enthusiastically, I hopped up from the laptop computer to go – and the wire that went from computer to wall snagged my ankle. I fell – this time forward. Again it was my straightened right arm that absorbed the brunt of the fall. It was excruciating. I pretended (*shake it off*) that it was nothing at all. I joined the walk to the Mayo Clinic (in a gusting, below-zero blizzard). I cradled my bent right arm in my good left hand.

We toured this magnificent facility, studied its unquestionably first-rate art – all of it the bounty of grateful donors. And yet, I was told, I could not make it through the doors without health insurance. A step into their emergency room might produce a $7,000 bill.

So I strolled through this iconic, celebrated medical facility that employs 30,000, clutching an arm that I thought was broken, and there was no one to help me. 'Iokepa and I whispered to one another behind the history exhibit, sharing the medical irony.

Our gathering that night was fabulous. If there reside in Minnesota folks who are less than gracious, warm, and welcoming, 'Iokepa and I have yet to encounter them. The morning afterwards, before we left for Winona on the shores of the frozen Mississippi River, I relented. I asked our nurse host to check my arm for a break. She did. It was not broken. But clearly my wrist needed to be immobilized. Her employer, the Mayo Clinic, wasn't her choice. She called her husband, an amiable physician's assistant at the Migrant Health Service, and asked him to help.

On our way out of town, we stopped at this unassuming, one-story building on the edge of the city. We were warmly received and we hunkered in among the migrant farm workers and their families in the bilingual waiting room.

'Iokepa's grandmothers have repeatedly instructed: "There's no such thing as a coincidence." Here's the evidence.

In Rochester, Minnesota, the home of the most prestigious medical complex on Earth, I was treated in the tiny, sparkling, human-scaled, Migrant Health Clinic. The treatment was exemplary, no red tape, no bureaucratic burden, and a perfunctory charge.

I was fitted with my choice of state-of-the-art wrist and arm braces. But here the story gets even more ironic – or what the engaging physician's assistant, our host called "the perfect story for you two."

"Only yesterday," he said with a mischievous grin, "my nurse and I went to the Mayo Clinic's warehouse. It's enormous. While we were leaving the warehouse, someone shouted to us: 'Here, take a box of these wrist braces, we have too many.'

"And *that's* the reason we have wrist braces for your arm today."

January 2008

What Holds Water?

We live in a noisy world.

We have coming at us in any given moment: telephones that no longer sit quietly next to our bed or on our office desks (they now follow our every step into movie theaters, churches, and romantic dinners with our lover); mail that no longer comes once a day on the eagerly awaited footsteps of our postman (now it beeps its electronic announcement night, day, and every moment between); news that no longer slaps at our doorstep at dawn or arrives from Walter Cronkite's lips at dusk (it comes at us 24/7 from so many contrary and irritating voices that it's hard to know whom to trust).

Yes, we can turn off the cell phone, the computer, and cable TV. But they remain a demanding, addictive call to arms. We are sorely afraid that we will miss something.

There was a time when we missed nearly everything, and never felt the loss. Never gave it a thought – so fully preoccupied were we with our immediate human relationships and the unavoidable life in our faces.

I can almost hear my elder son, some 6,000 miles away, laughing his head off at these thoughts. He is mocking my words – calling them *nostalgia*, accusing me of being an old geezer.

Permit me to clarify: mine is neither a judgment nor indictment of the abundant gifts of technology, the miracle of instant communication, the demanding world we've created.

But rather, how can we discern? How do we decide, among the Google of accessible information: *What holds water?*

Many years ago, the Hawaiian grandmothers told 'Iokepa: "When you've heard all the lies, you will know the truth." Daily, in these years, he has been strenuously tested.

There is so much knowledge, so little wisdom. In every niche of the internet, we find voices of ignorance that will affirm our own. There is no longer a need to be alone in our nightmares, fantasies, conspiracies, or falsehood. Everywhere there is a chat room or a website to keep us from feeling the occasional, well-deserved loneliness.

In the early days of cell phones – when it still felt outrageously intrusive to have the person standing in line with you at Starbucks answering classified ads or in the toilet stall next to yours arguing with a boyfriend – there was still the remaining hope of an agreed-upon civility.

'Iokepa used to laugh and say of that invasive cell phone usage: "Yes, we *know* you're not alone. We *know* you have someone who will actually speak with you." It did, at times, sound like the point of it all.

So there is Rachel Maddow and there is Bill O'Reilly. There is Wikipedia and there is Amazon. Newspapers disappear but there is no escaping Google. Publishers and bookstores fold; Netflix flourishes. Choose your weapon.

We fill ourselves with endless trivia. We have no protective sensory screen. Infomercials pour into our ears and eyes, and then undigested, out of our mouths. It is a terrifying national version of the childhood game of *Telephone* – so many distortions in the repetition.

We repeat what we hear, but have no ability to explain what we have repeated. We are marionettes, and someone – many, many someones – are pulling the strings. We pass as literate when we are really puppets. We spout opinions that won't hold up to challenge. We heard it, we read it, and it *sounded* true. The plethora of source smothers any likelihood of independent observation or idea. How *do* we know what holds water?

Without exception, my authentic thoughts and feelings (mine, not Keith Olbermann's) emerge from complete silence: in my walks along a beach, down a country lane, or in an urban forest – those places where my gut drowns out the stuff my mouth spouts reflexively. My answers matter, it seems, only if they've traveled the full length of my looping intestine.

Yet I realize that even a walk in the park demands a certain confidence – and its corollary, courage. We must fully believe that we are capable of independent thought. Then we must exorcise the noise that passes for consensus and conventional wisdom, in favor of our own quiet knowing. 'Iokepa says: "We owe it to our souls."

If it holds up alone on top of the mountain, it will very likely hold water.

October 2009

Home Again

Don't get me wrong. We are grateful for the loud, echoing voices of genuine friendship and loving support we're hearing from across that big continent. They say: "I can imagine the joy you're feeling, home on your beloved Islands."

And from those from within our tiny Island: "I've missed you. Welcome home!"

I fear my response might be too ambivalent for their expectations.

It's been a full month since we set foot again – ten days shy of one year away – on our Hawai'i. I feel the pressing necessity to record the fresh rush of feelings.

In the first week we hid out in the comfortable home of dear friends who were away on business. We stepped outside, tentatively, to meet selected folk and were taken by surprise at the outpouring of gratitude for our journey.

In the second week I renewed my suntan. We pitched a tent under the blazing tropical sun at the beach park where we lived for many of those ten years of *grooming*. It's where we lived among the Native Hawaiian homeless and the residual behaviors of almost 150 years of legislated cultural oppression.

Before the birth of the *Return Voyage* journey – before we left the Islands to speak – we lived that oppression. We lived without home, food, or any predictable source of income. We were required to live alternative behaviors to that which surrounded us. We were required to live our faith, our deep connection to the ancestors' knowing, and to the land.

On our second week back, the beach park awakened in me all that 'Iokepa and I had lived then – all that we had surrendered. Week Two stirred deep remembered emotions. I spent five hours one morning, alone, in silent tears.

The pain of those early years (easy now to transmute into narrative) seared my heart. I looked around and felt the horror of families crowded into canvas shelter, trying to prepare children for school under an exposed public shower, without use of even the single broken toilet.

I was confronted fully with my then-required personal surrender: the loss of my family's cherished home, my 30-year collection of revered books, the kitchen where I'd entertained lavishly, the computer where I wrote daily, and of the identities I savored: devoted mother, author, workshop teacher, daughter, and friend – all history!

But after I remembered the searing pain and the heartbreak – witnessed and lived fully – something else emerged. It was gratitude.

I told 'Iokepa. "We are, at this moment (after a year absent), gifted with clarity. Our senses are sharpened – sight and smell, sound and touch – by the year spent elsewhere. This is a sacred time."

In our *third* week, we pitched our tent on the side of the mountain (cool at night, bright with stars). On that mountain we had incredible birdsong for conversation, momentarily shifting clouds for companionship, and a growing to near-full moon. In the splendor and renewed silence of the mountain (cell phones couldn't reach us, email was non-existent), I sifted the conflicting emotions that poured through my alert senses and complicated memories.

Now it is Week Four. We are living in the guest cottage on the breathtakingly fertile five acres of a friend who is away on vacation in France. Every morning we pick papayas, oranges, bananas, starfruit, grapefruit, and we eat all this freshness in a bowl or in a blended smoothie. In the afternoon we pick avocados and snack on guacamole. In the evening we gather our lettuce and kale and spring onions from the garden, and collect a few eggs from those fat and sassy Rhode Island Reds.

Every few minutes I lay down the book I'm reading (*Dreams from My Father*, by Barack Obama), and I stroll these incredible orchid-filled acres. Today, I'm writing once again.

Over these four weeks, the question has remained the same: What is it that I mean by *home*? Why can't I satisfy our friends and write simply and with pure reverie about the glories of being home? Today, the answers emerge.

In the early morning I walked these acres (knowing that today was the day I would begin to write my thoughts). I prayed, as I do, before I sit down and put words on the page: "*Ke 'I'oakua* – God Almighty – ancestors of this land, give me the words."

This is what I heard.

These trees I walk among, the ocean I swim in, the sky I study, the fruit I eat – they are my real home, but only in this moment. That magnificent Lake Superior last January was my home – at that moment – and the Mississippi delta in Louisiana, one month later. The alligator babies with the anhinga perched above them in the Everglades were home last February. The piercing gorge of the Grand Canyon was my home last March. The foothills of Eastern Missouri, rife with red-bud, my home last April.

Home is, of necessity, momentary, fleeting. But always, it lies in our fundamental connection to the natural world. So home demands awareness. *Home* doesn't gift itself without our conscious choice to notice it – to know it. We mistake all the wonderful people in our lives for home. Where they live, we call home.

I am told that they – our loving mothers, our at-odds teenage sons, our present or absent husbands, our friends who we-can-call-in-the-middle-of-the-night – are the powerful human community who give us comfort (or not). But these relationships are never our source. They are at times comforting, at times the opposite. The human community (and our varied relationships within it) is where our hearts and souls are challenged to grow into our truest selves, where we become deepening shades of the heart and soul of our Creator.

But it is, and always will be, the natural world where we find home. We will find it only in that moment when we stand still among the trees or on a riverbank, at the edge of a cliff or near a pod of dolphins.

So, every moment of this year with 'Iokepa – in the desert of Albuquerque and the Blue Ridge Mountains of Virginia, on the Atlantic coast of

Delaware and Central Park in the heart of Manhattan – I was most certainly home.

And yes, here within this culture that we speak about so lovingly, on the land that is filled with my husband's ancestors' bones, I am brimming with joy and comfort and gratitude to be home.

September 2008

"What Would You *Do* with Your Freedom?"

This is the insistent (seldom kindly spoken) challenge that 'Iokepa Hanalei 'Īmaikalani hears whenever he dares to speak of the future of the Native Hawaiian people – or of their nation. The implied conclusion is: these people would not know what to do with their sovereignty. The implied assertion: deny them that choice.

'Iokepa answers the question in a larger way.

He begins by reminding me of a single moment last May. We sat, just the two of us, snug inside our Toyota Camry at a bed-and-breakfast parking lot in Rehoboth Beach, Delaware. We were six months into our second speaking tour, with perhaps three more to go.

We had $100 in our pockets. We'd just been informed that access to our Bank of Hawai'i checking account was shut down – the account had been drained with a pirated debit card. We had no pre-existing plan; we'd made no firm commitments. In that single moment we asked one another and the universe, "Where to next?"

'Iokepa focuses on that moment of possible anguish and uncertainty to make his point: "In that parking lot in Delaware, we were free. There were absolutely no demands made of us. We could go anywhere we wanted."

In that moment, I chose to go to Maine. We'd never before been to New England; we knew not a single soul; it simply felt right. I could not have offered a rationale that would have satisfied anyone I know – except 'Iokepa, who like me, asks out loud and then *listens.* We honor the answer we hear in our heads, our hearts, and our guts.

From my impromptu decision to drive onto the Interstate and head for the northernmost state on the Eastern seaboard, with just the barest possibility of gas money, and none for lodging – life delivered abundance.

Oh, the stories I could tell of Maine and beyond: the out-of-the-blue cell phone call from a friend in Hawai'i ("You're in Maine?! M*y* family lives there – let me call them."); or the dentist who repaired my newly broken tooth, gratis; or the clarity of purpose that unfolded from my freely made choice.

'Iokepa says: "People don't believe that kind of freedom is attainable. They can't imagine it for themselves. They can't fathom that anyone can live a life without allowing external demands to limit their choices. They don't believe it's possible."

But it is real – for every single one of us. The only demand that matters is the one that comes from deep within us. All choice is our own; it is our human default setting.

We are free unless and until we agree to hand our freedom over. We are enslaved only when we give up that freedom on someone else's say-so. Nelson Mandela may well have been the singular freest human who ever breathed – in prison for half a lifetime. On the other hand, most of us walk the streets in chains. We answer phones, take vacations, and never breathe a free moment in our lives.

The challenge remains – for the Native Hawaiians, *sure* – but no less for each one of us who walk this good Earth: "What will we do with our freedom?

November 2009

Grandmothers Whisper Wins

Like all good stories, this one has a beginning, middle, and an end.

After thirteen years writing and rewriting, drafting and re-drafting, *Grandmothers Whisper* found its miraculous way to a bound book that could actually be held in your hands (or alternatively downloaded onto your Kindle) just last Thanksgiving.

I've written books before, but never anything like this one. This book was scribbled across scores of legal pads, praying always that the paper and the ink would hold out because there was never money enough to replace them. It was written on dirty picnic tables in county parks, and inside cramped tents bent over a flashlight.

When *Grandmothers Whisper* finally struggled against odds to publication – after a powerful literary agent encountered a series of rejections because it fell through the marketing *niche* cracks, neither *this* nor *that* – the depth of my appreciation and sense of accomplishment was naturally commensurate with the obstacles overcome, greater than for anything I'd written before.

'Iokepa and I committed ourselves to six months, grass-roots, car travel – lugging cartons of the book in the trunk and on the backseat of our Camry. We felt we *owed* that book tour to the folks who had buttressed our work on behalf of the aggrieved Native Hawaiian people and their impressive culture.

These people, who'd paved our way in so many different ways, live on all the Islands and in every corner of the U.S. continent. They've housed us, fed us, and hosted *Return Voyage* gatherings over the years. We wanted to bring the finally-bound book to their cities, towns, and neighborhoods in the most personal way we could. It has been six months now, and we have been good to our word.

Last December 17, we began the book tour in New York City at the New York Open Center where we spoke to men and women in turbans, saris, blue jeans, mini-skirts – with dialects that originated from across the planet. Very slowly, we found our way down the edge of the East Coast to Siesta Key, Florida. A well-read friend mentioned we might want to present our book at a "fine" bookstore nearby, in Sarasota. I sent an email to the Google generic bookstore address and received an answer from a woman named Kim who said: "I'm not the buyer; I can't make a decision to stock the book." That, we assumed, was the end of that.

But instead, *that* only launches the middle of this story.

Several days later, this Kim person had read the book, emailed us that she loved it – and invited us to lunch with her. Free for the day, we agreed. We assumed that Kim was a clerk.

When we walked next door to the restaurant, I asked: "Kim, exactly what is your job here?" She laughed and said, "My best friend and I started the store twenty years ago. I'm the owner."

"And you aren't the buyer?" I asked. "No," she laughed. "My partner and I are still best friends because we do different jobs – and we don't interfere with one another."

We had this lunch and conversation last January. At that lunch, the owner of this splendidly imaginative and capably-run bookstore told us that she believed in *Grandmothers Whisper*; that we *must* attend something called the International New Age Trade Show (INATS) in Denver in late June.

Neither 'Iokepa nor I had ever heard of this trade show for spiritual publishers, bookstore owners, and authors. We had planned to be home in May. We hesitated.

In the next few days, Kim (an incredibly convincing businesswoman, in addition to being a genuinely fine human being) had – on our behalf – reserved a hotel room at the conference; booked us as seminar speakers; and arranged a *Grandmothers Whisper* book signing at the event.

Finally, she convinced us to enter the book in a national competition for a "Best of Year 2011 Visionary Award." Done. We committed ourselves to attending this three-day event in late June in Denver.

We continued our tour: Florida to Louisiana, Louisiana to New Mexico, New Mexico to Missouri, Missouri to Minnesota, Minnesota to North Carolina, to Virginia, to Maryland, to Delaware, and back to New York again.

The story ends here.

This past weekend we were – as promised – in Denver on our way west and then home to Hawai'i.

On Saturday morning, June 25, we walked into the expansive INATS exhibit hall inside the sprawling Denver Merchandise Mart. We couldn't make out the limits of the room because it was teeming with thousands of booksellers, book buyers, and simply curious book lovers. It was hard to see over their heads. There were several hundred display booths arranged in rows that showcased the impressive wares of major publishers, book distributors, and lesser known vendors of the gizmos and gadgets that fill bookstore shelves. We found our way to the dead-center of the exhibit floor for our scheduled one-hour book signing.

It was our first clue that this would not be an ordinary day. The line to get a copy of, and our signatures on, *Grandmothers Whisper* stretched out of our sight and into the distant corner of the hall. It never got shorter. People who staffed display booths snuck away to stand in line. After two hours, we ran out of books – but never of line or conversation. The enthusiasm for the grandmothers' words did not abate.

We had, and still have, no idea how these strangers knew about our book. Apparently the INATS community was pretty tight.

When the book boxes emptied, I was emptied as well – exhausted. My brain was pounding with the crowd's noise; my new dress shoes were slicing at my feet. "Find me a quiet place to sit," I begged 'Iokepa. "I'm finished!"

But it was just the beginning of our day. 'Iokepa led me to an empty meeting room at considerable distance from the overwhelming exhibit hall, and offered me a half an hour of silence and a sandwich. Then we headed to our seminar (named by trade show organizers), "Aboriginal Hawaiian Culture as the Perfect Business Model." Running a so-called spiritual bookstore asks something more than usual of a proprietor. The Hawaiian culture has a lot to say about community, of course, about how we treat one another other – in this case, employees and customers.

Our new friend, blond and radiant Kim sat in the first row. Afterwards she said: 'The room changed during your seminar – your energy and enthusiasm connects people to one another. You touch hearts." To us, it felt real and it felt satisfying.

But it left us with just a half-hour to return to our hotel room and get changed for the awards dinner. Anticipating this event last March at a discount store in Virginia, I'd bought a pretty spiffy suit to wear. The skirt was black; the jacket was boldly zebra striped with a trim at the hips in shocking pink flowers.

We raced to the hotel, did the quick change: I pushed a comb through my hair, a Kleenex over my shining nose, and a tube of lipstick across my lips. We *ran* from the hotel (my feet still aching), hurled ourselves across the exhibit hall, and entered the double doors to the awards dinner.

'Iokepa and I stopped in our tracks. The dazzling dining room under crystal chandeliers was spread over three elevated tiers filled with large round tables. Each table was set for eight;

the three levels seated more than 1,000. Every table was covered with handsome zebra-striped tablecloths, complete with shocking pink napkins.

I was, it appeared, indistinguishable from the table-settings. What were the chances?!

Well, perhaps a few folks might see some smoke-signals, signs, and portents here. I just thought it was incredibly funny. It had been a wonderful day, meeting bright and intriguing men and women, and now I was dressed like the table-settings.

An hour later, the emcee called out the second runner-up, and then the first runner-up among the hundreds submitted by their big-name publishers – and then he enunciated *Grandmothers Whisper* and my name perfectly. The book cover flashed in front of us on a huge screen next to the stage.

And so, the book, written on red-dirt spattered paper on the beaches of Hawai'i, had won a "Best of Year 2011 Visionary Award," and the crowd in that room jumped to its feet and erupted with a single deafening roar of approval.

I don't remember much else. 'Iokepa spontaneously stood and chanted in the language of his ancestors. His reverberating chant silenced the roar. I was handed an imposing, sixteen-inch, black onyx obelisk weighing (it felt at the time) like ten pounds. It was exquisitely engraved, chiseled in white.

Apparently, at the podium I managed to say: "*Mahalo* Grandmothers."

The black obelisk is being shipped home to Kaua'i. We will follow in a few weeks.

June 2011

Power to the Reader!

It's a very funny thing about being a writer. I complete a book. I've said everything that I have to say about the matter. Then the book tour begins and I am expected to say more – much more. When the questions commence, silence is just not an option – not on radio, not on TV, not in print.

Writing the book, *Grandmothers Whisper* was completely in my hands. But my control stopped there. I cannot pretend to know how any single human heart or mind will respond to reading my memoir. I do know that each of us brings our own story to bear on the one we read on the page.

Love it, hate it, read into it, or read out of it – in the silence of the reader's living room, I have no problem. Only in the public arena – the arena of public opinion and publicity (so the potential reader knows the book exists) – does interpretation become daunting.

If you heard 'Iokepa or me being interviewed in Detroit, Minneapolis, Atlanta, Central California, or in Ontario, Canada (by phone and in person) in a single day (and this did actually happen a couple days ago) – you would have sworn that you had heard us speak about five completely different books.

In Atlanta, the book was emphatically described by the interviewer as a wonderful love story – a story of destiny fulfilled in the merging of two strangers at a sacred Native Hawaiian site on Christmas morning nearly fifteen years ago.

But in Minneapolis, the host challenged the *craziness* of a woman who irresponsibly, without good-enough reason, abandoned a perfectly wonderful life in Portland, Oregon to selfishly drag her fourteen-year-old son to hardship and destitution on Hawaiian beaches.

In Central California it was determinedly the account of Native Hawaiians, who, within their ancient matriarchal culture, offered answers to our modern, warring world.

In Detroit, however, this book was about personal freedom, about what constitutes wealth or poverty, and about oppression – all oppression.

And in Canada – God bless those wonderful Canadians – my memoir was about *simplifying* ones life, about the stuff we accumulate, about a woman and man who live quite well, thank you, owning only what we carry in the trunk of our car.

That was just within a single day.

On another day, it looked like this: a Jewish woman, who discovered her own beliefs and culture via her immersion into her husband's (of all things!) indigenous Hawaiian culture.

On still another, the interviewer said the book is about *relationship*: our relationship to change (do we fear it?); our relationship to intimacy (do we fear it?); our relationship to our children (do we fear for them?).

'Iokepa and I are asked to anticipate each of these lines of inquiry. We are expected to imagine what a single reader might bring to our story to make it his or her own. As the ancestral grandmothers say about life itself, "Everything and anything can change in a breath."

Never do we contradict a well-intentioned reader's attempt to join the story at the place where it touches her heart or mind, emotion or intellect. The solemn fact of the matter is this: Every single thing that has been said about *Grandmothers Whisper* is true. The words on its pages are now the reader's story. We hope that she follows them, fearlessly, wherever they take her.

May 2012

In Solitude

'Iokepa Hanalei 'Īmaikalani and I live a life that is at odds with the person that I am – and yet it is not. This life, as he and I live it, addresses only one half of me – the half that communicates meaningfully with other humans. My very destiny is caught up with the skill, the need, the *substance* of words – speaking them aloud, writing them aloud in the hearing of other ears. Both fulfill me amply; it is my nature.

I grew up in a family that encouraged exactly that. We spoke our thoughts and our feelings. We were rewarded for being social – and we worried over the family members who did not share the skill. There was no praise for being a bump on the log. There was no praise for an interior life. *That* life might not show up appropriately on a face or in the sparkle of your eyes.

So I have been well-trained in the manner of social interaction – and maybe I took to it like a duck to water. But it most certainly does not define the whole of me, although through much of my early life, I didn't know the difference. But the difference is huge – and somewhere around age forty I came to understand that.

From college until thirty-five, I occupied myself with daily journalism: words spoken from my reporter's mouth to others' ears; words spoken from others' mouths to my ears. I recorded all these words on many pages over the years, and I got paid to do it.

Then there were the early years with children: five years buried in the heart of Southern Appalachia on a forty-five-acre farm that sat at the end of innumerable connecting and increasingly diminishing roads through mountains and valleys to our driveway. I lived those years in isolation from the social. I reared babies; I grew potatoes and I grew asparagus, apples, and plums. I took blue-prize ribbons at the state fair bake-offs for apple pie and strawberry shortcake. I fed parts of myself that I didn't know that I contained.

But ultimately, that isolation – the lack of human society, of words spoken and words received – tore at my very fiber, and the marriage ended.

Then, somewhere around age forty, the balance between my contradictory impulses was struck.

I surrendered both the farm's isolation and my earlier family social programming, too. I moved with my sons to a neighborhood in a small city. I put my sons on the school bus at 8:00 a.m. and lifted them off at 3:00 p.m. – and in between I sat in silence at my roll-top desk in a glass room that I designed for the purpose, and I wrote.

For thirteen years alone with my sons, I wrote books – long treatises examining my own life and the lives around me. Then, after 3:00 p.m. and on weekends, I engaged humanity via children on the soccer field and Hebrew school and birthday parties; via the neighbors and a writing workshop that I taught; via television appearances – book promotion.

I struck a balance. I walked trails on the Blue Ridge Parkway in Virginia. I later walked the shores of the Oregon Coast. I had deep friendships – and seven hours a day, for at least five days a week, I had solitude.

Then 'Iokepa Hanalei 'Īmaikalani entered my life with his "prophecy," his life force, and his destiny. I met this Native Hawaiian man whose very being defines "extrovert" – who *fills* and who feeds from humanity, who finds enormous strength from the exchange of ideas with other humans.

I met a man who many call charismatic. He bleeds interest in others – he listens with an intensity that is rare, and he speaks with a commitment to his own truth that is riveting. And I (like many others) was drawn into his world. *Grandmothers Whisper* tells the story of those first ten years in tents – a life without walls that either protect privacy or insure silence.

What it does not tell is the story of the life that has followed: these even less private *Return Voyage* years, the years of taking what we lived and learned and speaking about them across the American continent – almost never alone, never without talk.

But now I am writing these words under a hand-stitched quilt, inside an 1810 farmhouse, on 180 acres stretched along a mile and a half of the Shenandoah River, in the valley of the same name. I am propped on flannel-covered pillows, gazing through windows that frame hills rising from the riverbank, in a room without curtains or "window treatment." There is no need for them.

There are Canadian geese within my sight line at a pond that lies between me and the river. There isn't another house in view. There are perfectly maintained wooden fences for cattle that are absent during these months. There is a barn just outside my window frame that houses at the moment a single horse.

'Iokepa is down in the kitchen at breakfast, and I have been given the gift of solitude, of personal privacy, of utter and total silence. This simple space (empty of a single thing that feels *extra*) has been newly renovated to perfection, and the pantry filled with the food we love.

We are the first people to live in this newly refreshed house. We share it only with the spirit of a much earlier inhabitant.

This farm is the gift of a woman who heard us speak at a bookstore in Winchester, Virginia, over a month ago on a book tour that took us in that month to Pittsburgh and Baltimore, to Richmond and Asheville, to Sarasota and Atlanta.

It has been an intense, exhausting, and remarkably rewarding series of appearances at bookstores, clubs, and churches throughout the Southeastern United States. It has used us – used me – well. It has served my nature, my need to communicate, my need to exchange words with other humans. But it has starved me as well.

We appreciate always the hospitality offered in the guestrooms of our many wonderful hosts, and we know how to be good guests. We move about on their schedules, attempt not to intrude; clean up after ourselves – of course.

I sit now in a home that is solely ours this week – or for whatever time we can spare of ourselves from scheduled events: speaking out and telling stories, chanting, and answering questions.

So in the midst of these engaging months and years – sharing homes and meals and conversation that last well into the night – we received an email from this stranger and her newly renovated, totally unoccupied farmhouse. She is a farm woman who has "taken in critters" all her life. She intuited (sitting there listening to me read in that bookstore) a need in the midst of this intense and homeless travel of ours – and she offered this.

And *this*, on the banks of the Shenandoah River, where the maples and oaks are leafless in winter, my heart and soul are full of the sounds of silence.

February 2012

All for a Good Story

Okay, so this is what I remember of the story I'm about to tell: absolutely nothing. It's a black hole of a story, but it is quite a story nevertheless, as 'Iokepa slowly reveals it to my still erratic (but getting sharper every day) Swiss cheese of a memory bank.

The "Before"

After several bookstore events in Monterrey and Carmel, we were headed up the California coastline. I remember a three-night stop in Ukiah at a Travelodge Motel – some sunshine and a swimming pool. The rest goes dark to amnesia.

But I am told that on this day, May 20 (the day of the solar eclipse), 'Iokepa and I (in our beloved black Camry with the gold wheels) decided on the coastal route to Oregon. The intention was a slow, two-day drive, with a one-night stop in Grants Pass, and then up to Portland for our next book event. We got, I'm told, as far as the giant redwoods when the trip was abruptly halted.

In these past years we have covered 95,000 car miles in that 1998 black Camry with the sunroof, the grey leather interior, the spoiler, and the gold trim that was gifted to us with 89,000 miles on it, four and a half years ago for this purpose. In Ukiah (last stop) it still looked exactly as if it just rolled off the showroom floor.

Such was the tender loving care of my husband. Such was the care of the couple in Washington State who bought it new. A day didn't pass without someone, somewhere asking about that unusually beautiful car, and then registering shock when told it was fourteen years old.

The purpose of that gift, the car we called *Dark Horse*, was simple: to share the Hawaiian ancestors' lives, as well our journey on their paths.

What we have is a good story. And frankly, all my life I've been a sucker for a good story. Maybe that's why I first fell in love with 'Iokepa these fourteen and a half years ago. He had a whopper of a story.

In any case, I'd worked my entire life as a reporter, listening and re-telling other people's stories – occasionally, my own. *Grandmothers Whisper* is my own – and it is also the story of an indigenous people who at their best (which, these days, is not every day nor in all ways) remember that which all of us once knew but may have forgotten.

The "Now"

Forgotten – like me, right now. I have completely forgotten (since we left that motel in Ukiah) the car heading toward ours on narrow Highway 199 in Jedediah Smith Redwood Park, driven by a young man – who'd been released from prison four hours before and was now highly inebriated and driving 80 mph in a 40 mph zone. I have forgotten his Honda, which crossed the center line and plowed into the driver's door of our pristine Camry (my husband averted the head-on in those last breaths to spare me). I have forgotten the force of that Honda, which crushed my Camry door into one of the awe-inspiring colossal redwoods with a six-foot diameter.

I remember nothing.

'Iokepa blacked out briefly, but he remembers every single detail. He wondered for just a moment whether he were still alive. He remembers being encircled by the first witnesses – a group of tough motorcyclists, one step removed from the Hell's Angels. They were heavily cursing the other driver, who'd abandoned his car and run into the woods. I'll spare you their specific epithets.

'Iokepa remembers cradling my unconscious head, one huge hand behind my neck, the other under my jaw; and he remembers speaking words without let-up of love and comfort to my unconscious.

He remembers the arrival of the police and the fire department, the "jaws of life" extracting him first, then me, from that no-longer-beautiful Toyota Camry (now unfashionably svelte – nipped in at the waist), both sides compacted between the other car and the redwood. The front grill and hood remained shiny and recognizable. He remembers everything we own in the world, save for a closet full of camping gear still on the Island, now strewn across the road and among the hovering trees.

He remembers the ambulance ride to the hospital and my apparently insisting to anyone who would or would not listen that, "'Iokepa is the best driver in the world – this wasn't his fault." Apparently, I'm given to understand, that repetition was my specialty in the hospital during the week that followed.

'Iokepa remembers the emergency room from 1:00 p.m. until 11:00 p.m. I kept asking him every thirty seconds, "Did you call my brother?" In all those hours 'Iokepa never left my side, never stopped attempting to comfort the only part of me he could safely massage – my feet – and assuring me of his love while answering again and again the drumbeat of my repeated questions. I was wheeled out and back for a CAT scan, MRI, x-rays, and much more.

He remembers too the names and faces of each and every attending medical person. He remembers being granted privileges – a bed next to mine in a room we would share in the Sutter Coast Hospital in the California coastal town of Crescent City.

My heroic husband (he refuses to acknowledge my use of that word) – who steered the car toward himself to spare me – spent every moment of every day in the hospital fielding the deluge of necessary communication in the midst of a national book tour away from home, our family and friends at great distance. 'Iokepa - who has consistently been the ambassador of everything that his people were and are at their very best – is considered "fine, unharmed, without a scratch." I know otherwise.

I have apparently surrendered six smashed ribs (front and back), one badly bruised lung, whiplash, a concussion, and memory loss to the cause. I get attention, flowers, candy, sympathy, compassion – prayers, meds, rest, and rehab.

'Iokepa gets paperwork, insurance companies, police reports, cancelled and rescheduled book tour events. He gets a wife who grows cranky when the day turns dim and the pain turns brighter.

We are both alive. We are both grateful. We are both absolutely certain that every bit of this unfolding is for a purpose. But that, I think, is another story, told another day. Please God, I will write that one as well.

For now, just this: My old literary agent told me many years ago, "Inette, you'll do anything for a good story." Just maybe she was right.

June 2012

These "Days of Awe"

For five autumns now, 'Iokepa and I have found ourselves strangers in unknown distant cities. Each year we've had to unearth a Jewish congregation from the yellow pages, and solicit an invitation to celebrate *Rosh Hashanah* and *Yom Kippur* in their large urban synagogue. Without exception, we've been embraced.

But it is here in our tiny Kaua'i Jewish Community that we find home. Blessedly, we are home again this year for these most sacred Days of Awe. Our little congregation – maybe sixty strong on a very good day, counting visiting tourists – can't afford a full-time rabbi, but we manage to bring one over for our High Holy Days each year. We don't own a building, but we share the Episcopal Church's breezy, glass-walled sanctuary on our separately observed Sabbaths and holidays. We make do.

We proudly celebrate our thirteen-year-old children's ritual coming of age, *bar* and *bat mitzvah*. We gather under the *chuppah* (canopy) for our tropical Jewish weddings. We sit *Shiva* (ritual mourning) when our members pass on. Like any cultural community, we share our joys and we share our grief. We share our traditions, never more emphatically than on these Days of Awe.

These ten days wedged between the Jewish New Year (Rosh Hashanah) and the Day of

Atonement (Yom Kippur) have always represented an opportunity to nudge what needs awakening in myself, to adapt to what demands change. It is a time of deep and profound self-examination, and I treasure these sacred days.

This year, as we come near to concluding these all-too-brief days that will end with a 24-hour fast, the opportunity for introspection feels especially profound.

So many have written and asked us: *Why* the car accident that could have so easily taken our lives last May 20, but instead took our Camry and my good health for these past four months. We have been e-mailed, phoned, and probed face to face by those who know our deep faith and our genuine belief that there really are no accidents in this life: "For what purpose?"

So in this week that defines the Jewish Days of Awe (that I'm blessed to have my *kanaka maoli* husband share), we sit in silence in synagogue and we sit in conversation at home and we ask ourselves, "For what purpose?"

The answer reveals itself, but I struggle to put it into words. Sometimes the deepest enigma is unveiled in the most overused phrases.

In sum: I am a better wife for this accident. I am a less judgmental human for this accident. I'm a more compassionate friend. I am more honest with myself. I cannot begin to say why that is so.

I realize – no, I physically *feel* the pain in my head, my neck, my chest, my arm, when I violate any of these claims. I hurt like hell when I fight, when I defend, when I win at another person's loss.

The flip side is that I'm less willing to spend the sum of my too-brief days – squandering them or me – on things that feel unimportant. I'm less willing to engage socially just because I should. I demand more honesty and meaning from both my words and my minutes.

So maybe it is true, as folks here like to laugh and say: "People don't move to the Hawaiian Islands to embrace their Judaism – they move to Brooklyn for that."

But it is here, on this most northwestern edge of the Hawaiian Island chain smack in the middle of the vast Pacific Ocean, that I welcome these Days of Awe, and that I find the answers to "For what purpose...?" in the arms and heart of my Jewish community.

September 2012

There Is More to the Good Story

It has been exactly one year since *Dark Horse* met the giant redwood. The car's fate was decided instantaneously. My full recovery – body and mind – took ten months.

The story that 'Iokepa and I tell now sounds different from the one I wrote then. The story we tell is the story of a community empowered, and therefore empowering. I'd be remiss not to repeat it here.

Crescent City, California – an aging coastal town with a total population of 7,652 sits just a few miles shy of the Oregon border. We spent two weeks post-wreck in its nurturing arms: the first in Sutter Coast hospital; the next, after discharge, in a nearby hotel.

Our association with the town and its huge-hearted people began with an untimely arrival by ambulance – destination emergency room. The emergency room doctor's *first* words to 'Iokepa were: "You think you're here because of the car wreck, but you're here for other reasons."

His next words: "I understand your car is totaled. I have an extra. You're headed to Seattle. My brother lives there. Use the car as long as you need it, and then drop it off at my brother's house."

And we did.

My injuries were complicated, and given the choice, many might have wished for a renowned university-affiliated medical center. I am grateful that I was not given that choice. The small community hospital defined compassion, care, and competence; medical "rules" were suspended for humane and human reasons. They left not a stone unturned to respond to 'Iokepa and my dislocation and need.

Here's short roster of the hospital staff's extracurricular generosity:

*A talented surgeon paid an unsolicited $300 out-of-pocket for pain-relieving patches that she knew were not covered by any insurance.

*A thoughtful doctor contributed a huge, hard-sided suitcase to replace our two smashed ones.

*Nurses and doctors lined up at the door of our room on our last day to buy up every single copy I had of *Grandmothers Whisper*, otherwise unsalable and damaged from the wreck, and to have them signed.

*A surgical nurse insisted after discharge that we visit her beautiful country home. Before dinner she massaged muscle spasms from my back and then served us a home-cooked meal in her garden.

*When my doctor heard that we were forced to spend an extra night in the hotel, she snuck into the hotel after work and paid our last night's bill before we could say 'no.'

But the hospital and its remarkable staff (caregivers by profession) defined only a single part of the embrace of Crescent City. There was much more.

Five days after the car wreck, I emerged from the worst of the amnesia, but my short-term memory remained impaired. The hospital public relations person asked 'Iokepa and me if we'd agree to be interviewed by the *Triplicate*, the local paper, and we did.

Remarkably I *remember* a bright, dark-haired young reporter, who was headed that fall to Columbia Journalism School. She enthusiastically pumped me for my exploits as a war correspondent at her age. Kelley Atherton wrote a full and sensitive story headlined: "Hiouchi Wreck Delays Pair's Nat'l Book Tour." It described our work, the book, and the heart of the Native Hawaiian culture.

It said in part:

> ...Early Sunday afternoon, the two were driving up U.S. Highway 199 through Hiouchi when they were struck head-on by a vehicle driven by (*my* substitution) John Doe. Doe fled on foot and was found later that afternoon, authorities said...
>
> ...Doe was arrested on suspicion of driving under the influence, hit-and-run causing injuries, and driving with a suspended license, authorities said...
>
> "Everything is for a purpose," Miller said. 'Imaikalani and Miller are adamant that they don't feel hate toward John Doe, but encourage the community to come together and support him so he can change his life. He

was recently released from jail after serving a sentence for assault.

Without a culture or sense of belonging to the community, "people act out and don't know how to control their actions," 'Īmaikalani said.

The foundation of a community is healthy people, 'Īmaikalani said. For thousands of years, tribes of people have taken responsibility for each person in the tribe and helped heal those who were struggling, he said.

In Hawaiian culture...the community was woven like a tapestry, Miller said, but nowadays so many people isolate themselves from other people or judge others for their indiscretions.

"It's not about making the person 'The other,'" she said, but to embrace him or her....

Before the newspaper story and photo from our book jacket appeared, the hospital had already been swamped with phone calls and drop-ins who had passed the crash site and were desperate for news of our well-being. The condition of Dark Horse made people fear the worst. Many strangers offered their homes for our convalescence.

After the newspaper story appeared on Thursday, 'Iokepa could not step into Safeway to buy a bit of comfort food or take a walk for fresh air without being approached by people who wanted him to know how much our words and message resonated.

"We have problems in our community," he was told. "We have drugs. No one has spoken as you and your wife have."

From the hospital, we were directed to the cozy and historic Lighthouse Inn to mend. The hotel, we knew, was beyond our means. But, in keeping with our embrace by Crescent City, the manager voluntarily halved his lowest price, and then offered us the largest suite in the hotel.

Furniture was moved for my mobility: a recliner was added and space was made for 'Iokepa to sort through our broken possessions. Everything we owned was full of glass.

Every day flowers awaited us at the front desk. These were bouquets from local gardens: lilacs aplenty. I struggle to remember more than being surrounded by the sweet scent of garden.

Every day there were trays of homemade chocolate chip cookies or brownies. When 'Iokepa walked the city's streets, he met no strangers. People recognized this Hawaiian with the long silver hair. Uniformly they approached him with concern and appreciation.

In our final few days, 'Iokepa passed though the doors of Safeway with a salad in hand. His exit was halted by the "best friend" of John Doe, who gently asked for a moment of his time. She was an attractive young woman with a warm smile and a forthcoming demeanor.

"Our mothers have been friends since we were babies," she said. She offered testimony to the man's goodness – a volunteer fireman; a man who was going through a hard time in the break-up of his marriage. He was in jail, and he wanted the chance to see us. 'Iokepa was non-committal. It was still exceedingly painful for me to move.

The next day a note arrived at our hotel, snuggled next to peonies and even more homemade desserts. The note told us: "'John Doe's' visiting hours are...."

'Iokepa said, "Of course, this is up to you."

We went.

The sheriff met us. He, too, was an advocate on John Doe's behalf: "I played football with him in high school. He is the best of men. I don't understand..."

We were admitted to the jail. The man who nearly killed me was awaiting us behind a thick glass window. His eyes widened as we entered, and no wonder. For here's what he must have seen: 'Iokepa, imposing, stern and fierce; and me, my every small and measured motion embedded with tremendous pain, stooped, unbalanced, supported by 'Iokepa and vulnerable.

My eyes widened too, because here's what I saw: a thirty-two-year-old man who could easily have been my own sensitive and handsome firstborn son. His blue eyes were brimming with tears. Visibly, he was full of remorse and impotence, in obvious pain of his own.

My words followed my heart. "You will *not* hate yourself on my behalf. I will be fine. All of us make mistakes; all of us screw up. It's what you do with what you learn here that matters.

"You're young. You have a long life ahead of you. I hate that you're in jail."

He answered, "I'm where I need to be, getting the help I need to get. I wasn't ready to get out when I was released."

He looked straight into my eyes – his, still full of tears – and he said, "You're beautiful."

We left the jail after 'Iokepa had spoken with him as well. 'Iokepa's first words were: "I'm not happy that you hurt my wife." And his last echoing words were: "Someday you and I will take a walk together." His clear implication was that John Doe would turn his life around. The young man nodded solemnly.

I needed to sit down on a low stone wall bordering the building, and rest; I was very tired and the sun on my face felt healing.

But in truth, *never* in my entire life have I felt so certain that I'd done the right thing – never. The light I sat under at that moment felt stronger by an immeasurable magnitude than mere sunshine could muster.

May 2013

"The Whole Earth Catalogue"

Ho'oponopono

This heading is more than a lovely Hawaiian word that rolls off the tongue like music. It is an even lovelier – or rather, a more potent – life-changing cultural mindset, by which the *kanaka maoli*, the aboriginal Hawaiians, will potentially instruct the world. It is the means by which these people refused the possibility of war for more than 12,000 years. Ours is a world sorely in need of some guidance.

By its smallest measure, *ho'oponopono* has been labeled an ancient Hawaiian mediation technique. By that narrow measure, western psychologists have discovered this ancient cultural gift (just as Captain Cook *discovered* the 13,000-year-old Hawaiian nation in 1778) and attempted to recast it to fit our modern sensibilities, and fill the vacuum of our spiritual satisfaction.

But ho'oponopono is much more than another twist and turn in the American academic competition to find a PhD dissertation topic. Psychological adaptations (and recent self-help books) have popularized ho'oponopono at the expense of truth, and to the disservice of the indigenous Hawaiian people.

Ho'oponopono cannot be lifted out of the deeply embedded context of the culture that birthed it. To embrace the ritual and to understand it in its fullness, one must wander deeply into the heart of these people, their language, and their history – must cut no corners.

Ho'oponopono is inseparably embedded in community. Aboriginal community is embedded, in turn, in their ancestors' spirit as manifest in every part of the natural world. There are no known shortcuts to building such a community. But living in one, we share a compassionate responsibility for one another and for every element of creation. That is the work to be done. It has been done before. It can be done again.

The alternative is an opportunity missed to bring peace to our warring Earth; to establish ease in the fearful angry hearts of our modern peoples; to recognize that our isolation from any aspect of nature – animal, mineral, and certainly human – wreaks destruction.

Ho'oponopono worked wonders on the Hawaiian Islands for thousands of years – during which time there were no wars, no gender segregation, and no hierarchy.

'Iokepa speaks of it often. "Ours was a matriarchal culture. Women gave birth. They believed that our Creator didn't need help in taking a life. Men honored that knowing. There were no wars.

"Only when a violent colonizing sect brought fear and denigration of women to our Islands in 1320 – and enslaved our open-hearted people – did our nation experience the aberration of war. War happens, when men cease to recognize that they are half their mothers – cease to embrace that wholeness. War is the mistaken search for that wholeness."

'Iokepa describes one possible result of ho'oponopono as a peacekeeping ritual. "When two young men wanted to fight, they were required instead to run a distance – not competitively, but together; then they had to swim a distance in the ocean together; then climb the mountain *together*. By the end of it, they had worked their energy down, and they realized that they sucked the same air."

At a New York Open Center gathering in Manhattan, a most-attentive participant, who spoke in the delightful lilt of his native Africa, extracted a promise. Time had run short; the evening ended without fully answering his questions about ho'oponopono. I promised to rectify the omission.

I begin with the "mediator." Always a woman, she was universally recognized and trusted for her commitment to the whole of the community. She was, by necessity, drug-and-alcohol-free; her connection to the divine required clarity.

The job demanded that she facilitate the healing of spirit – individually and communally. She did not mete out punishment.

Ho'oponopono – the ritual mediation at the heart of the aboriginal culture – demanded that every man and woman in a community examine his or her heart for complicity in every other human's misfortune: illness, emotional distress, physical harm. It had nothing to do with guilt. When we genuinely live these connections, we naturally assume responsibility for every living thing.

A community gathered to examine and clear its collective soul in this way. All members of the community sat in a circle – always with food. The trusted mediator held sway with a lidded gourd. When she lifted the lid off the gourd, the ritual began; when she returned the lid, it ended.

Simple enough: a circle, some food, a gourd, and a mediator. But – free of a community that deeply respects every life as a piece of his own life – the circle, the gourd, and the mediator are empty symbols.

And free of the setting – feeling the wind, hearing the sound of the ocean, watching the changing clouds, and then reading these elements and accessing their messages – there is no ho'oponopono. Finally, there is this all-important acknowledgment: gratitude for our ancestors' answers.

So ho'oponopono is not how we build community; it is how we support existing community. The trust, the clarity, and the purity of intent are the essential foundation for the ritual. Without that solidity of community and trust between souls, ho'oponopono is meaningless.

In a circle of kindred spirits, it might work like this. A man voices the distress he's experiencing in his household. Maybe the source is a son, a wife, or a mother-in-law – ill, or troubled in some less tangible way. Each person in the communal circle takes time to examine his or her own heart for complicity in that trouble, and in turn (at the prompting of the mediator) speaks it.

Perhaps I'm a neighbor, sitting in that circle. I feel in my heart, and then speak aloud when my turn comes. "Last week, when your son called my son 'stupid,' I felt anger toward both of you. I'm part of your troubles. I ask your forgiveness."

In the days after this ritual, the entire community slows their ordinary activities to heal the troubling breach. Without a full healing, the community is not whole.

Every word or action within community impinges on every other. Each soul and each element of nature either nurtures or refuses (for one reason or another) to nurture the rest. Ho'oponopono is an opportunity to claim responsibility for our thoughts, our actions, and give ourselves (and others) a chance at peace.

That cannot be done without the hard work, first, of building a responsible, integrated community and fully acknowledging the divine thread that sustains every aspect of it. That – now – is the work of the world.

June 2008

In the Heart of the Ojibwa Nation

Our road atlas has two full-page maps of Minnesota: one south and one north. But the top of that northern map stops short of a chunk of Minnesota that wraps still *further* north and east around the largest lake on Earth, Lake Superior. Tucked elsewhere on the atlas page, we located an insert that continued the job up to Canada.

That is where we've spent this past week – about a quarter of a map inch from the Canadian border, in the winter wonderland of Hovland. Imagine a Native Hawaiian experiencing nightly saunas followed by dips in the icy January waters of Lake Superior, and you begin to picture how powerfully different – yet remarkably the same – this week has been.

Lake Superior has 2,730 miles of shoreline. It covers 31,280 square miles. At its deepest, it is over a quarter of a mile deep. Sitting on its shoreline, watching waves crash against the rocks – it felt an awful lot like an ocean.

Yes, we saw bald eagles soaring – exotic to our Island eyes – but we also felt a silent communion with water, Earth, and element that was familiar. True, the water was fresh, not salt; and these were eagles, not our albatross. But the place exuded a spiritual power that was kindred, and very soothing.

Grand Portage Indian Reservation, home to the Ojibwa, straddles the U.S. and Canadian national borders here.

"My friends want to know," Bob SwanSon, Ojibwa elder and poet, asked 'Iokepa this week, 'What's an indigenous Hawaiian doing so far inland?'"

'Iokepa answered: "I'm retracing the steps of my ancestors."

For thousands of years, aboriginal Hawaiians sailed the Pacific in their sophisticated canoes – and integrated into the indigenous culture up and down the Americas. "There is a kinship," 'Iokepa said. "What we see in one another is familiar and yet we're eager to learn what's different." These people were not strangers to 'Iokepa.

So when three Ojibwa natives honored our *Return Voyage* gathering at Hovland with their attendance, a few nonverbal similarities surfaced. When 'Iokepa spoke to the gathering, Bob SwanSon, solemn and silent, kept his eyes lowered to the floor. Afterwards, several non-native participants remarked, "I thought Bob was sleeping."

But the thought never crossed either my mind or 'Iokepa's. We *felt* the depth of Bob's listening and focus. He looked at the floor (as I sometimes do when 'Iokepa is speaking) to screen out all other sensory distraction, and to truly listen. It's the indigenous way.

Still later, one non-native woman observed: "The Native Americans don't meet your eyes when they speak."

"I've found the opposite," I answered. "Most seem to read you quickly. If there's authenticity within you, they recognize it – and if there's not, they see that too. They look deeply and they leave me feeling known. "

But that requires patience. We must learn to sit easily with a silence that many of us refuse. Indigenous are not afraid of silence. They listen to it deeply for the answers to their prayers.

'Iokepa typically looks intently into the eyes of men and women – and occasionally they say that they feel vulnerable and exposed. But I think that has less to do with what he sees, and far more with how we see and judge ourselves.

In fact, we needn't fear either silence in the presence of one another – or that silence unveiling our truest selves.

January 2008

From Native Heart to Native Mind

We first met John Talley at an Eastside Portland coffee shop called *Common Grounds*. He was sitting one table away and couldn't help overhearing 'Iokepa speaking with an old friend. John was intrigued by what he heard, introduced himself, and apologized for eavesdropping.

'Iokepa, for his part, was drawn immediately to the seventy-six-year-old Iroquois with the powerful face – etched deeply along strong native features – and the gentle voice. They agreed to meet again.

'Iokepa arrived at that meeting with a packet of sea salt, harvested from *Kaheka* – the Salt Pans on Kaua'i. The Salt Pans are a rare geological phenomenon, but they are more. Sea salt has been harvested there under the strictest of ancient ritual and tradition, by the same native families for thousands of years. Salt was, and is, a vital part of Hawaiian life.

"I bring you an offering," 'Iokepa said to John. "We're walking now on your land and the land of your ancestors. For thousands of years my ancestors voyaged here to integrate with your people – never to teach them, never to change them."

John said, "The Indian and the Hawaiian message is much the same. The details vary. The needs of our people are the same."

The common ground was fertile.

John Talley's native name is Talks on the Wind. "I see changing winds. I see growth in our native peoples – finding their way back."

'Iokepa answered, "In the Hawaiian language, we have 160 words for the wind; each one speaks to a subtle difference. The wind blows through you, like a ticker-tape full of knowledge. Our work is about change."

John added, "And the simpler your lifestyle, the less likely you'll be crushed by the winds of change."

For thirty-two years, John Talley produced an Oregon radio show called *Indian World*. ("We were trailblazers.") He invited 'Iokepa to be the featured guest on his show. John introduced 'Iokepa to his listeners like this. "Hear this man, my brothers and sisters, because his people have been through the same oppression we have. The fortunes of war have brought a lot of people under the flag who never asked to be brought there. It's something American Indians know well."

'Iokepa spoke. "In my culture we have answers to questions that plague the world today. It's about remembering how to ask – and how to listen for the answer. In our language, there are 138 words for the rain. Knowing the differences between each wind and each rain was about survival. Three thousand miles out in the Pacific, you had to know.

"At the end of each day that you were given breath, you offered gratitude. That gratitude became ritual and ceremony."

John answered. "I'm so glad that you spoke that way. There is something very disturbing about some in the American Indian community *selling* ceremony. It's very wrong! Performing ceremony is fine – but selling it . . . *never.*"

'Iokepa said, "All people have birth knowledge – *'ike hānau.* Our work is to bring us back to the things we already know but may have abandoned."

John responded, "My grandmother said the same thing: 'We're born with all the knowledge in the universe, and then the world tramples us down.'"

'Iokepa: "And yet we all have an immense genealogy to draw on. It's time to speak out. We have to be heard. We must come together to heal ourselves and to heal this Earth."

John spoke of the pain and the confusion. "There are times I don't see that mountain out there for months. It's hidden behind the clouds. But it's there whether I see it or not. The solutions are sometimes not visible for the clouds. But the solutions *are* there."

'Iokepa spoke of the healing. "The indigenous peoples knew that they were not separate from all living things. But we no longer live with the elements – we live against them. Our ancestors named their children after the elements; the names spoke of his or her destiny. Each of us has unique gifts. We must honor one another for those gifts."

"John: "Yes!"

'Iokepa: "And we need to *use* our gifts. We look up at the sky and we think we're so small – too small to make a difference. But we're all part of the universe, and we must accept our part. Too often, we listen only to other people's words – written or spoken. We must listen to our own."

October 2007

Pure Science Meets Pure Spirit

Many years ago now, our first years together, 'Iokepa and I were living in a tent at the Salt Pans Park on Kaua'i, when we met Lou Pignolet and his wife Inger, who were also camping there.

Over the years we met many hundreds of visitors to the Island on that particular beach: some there for a quick swim by day; others camping for a week. They were vacationing from Germany, Canada, Switzerland, Denmark, Austria, Australia, the Netherlands, Japan, and every part of the United States.

But Lou and Inger struck up a provocative conversation that continues to this day. Lou was then head of the Chemistry Department at the University of Minnesota. He was a low-key, soft-spoken, brilliant scientist – a dedicated teacher.

I don't remember who engaged whom first, but neither 'Iokepa nor Lou would have shirked the challenge of a passionate, thoughtful exchange.

'Iokepa spoke, as he does always, from ancestral prodding. I remember Lou, middle-aged and extremely fit, being respectful and I remember him being full of important questions. Apparently, during his annual visits to the Island, he had developed an unquenchable thirst for the truth of the indigenous culture.

At one point, 'Iokepa launched into a riff about the power of our ancestral connection. He held up his arms, spread wide over his head, and said: "Everything your ancestors lived, now comes down to *you*." He drew his hands into a funnel shape and held them over Lou's heart. "You carry all that they lived in your DNA."

At that moment I cringed. *No, 'Iokepa!* I thought, but did not say. *You don't talk DNA to a scientist, a chemist...an academic.* I looked at Lou with trepidation. He answered with a big grin. "That makes perfect sense."

It was the beginning of our friendship. This year, Lou weighed in by mail: "I'm recommending a book, *The Field,* even though it's everything 'Iokepa already knows and lives. But this one's written in the language that I speak."

It is the work of a reputable British science writer. The author, Lynne McTaggart, explores and reports on scientific attempts, in a dozen prestigious laboratories around the globe, to measure and define the spiritual paths that 'Iokepa and I walk daily. This is the scientific method applied to everyday miracles.

Thankfully, I feel no need to convince anyone of anything. Each of us is fully capable of discerning our own measure of what is true. What I love about the friendship between 'Iokepa and Lou is that neither of them looks at the other as *not me*. Neither believes that it's a matter of science *or* the aboriginal wisdom. Both know that what the ancients lived (because they were so connected to the elements), scientists try to replicate in the controlled setting of a laboratory.

I say: blessings on both their endeavors.

November 2007

Racism 101

Racism: it's in no way subtle. But neither is it consistent. There are ironies that would be laughable if they weren't so painful. Like a bad joke, it only hurts when I laugh.

So our president, Mr. Barack Obama – whose mother hails from Kansas and whose father was the son of an African tribal chief (making our president by any mathematical calculation *half* white and *half* black, and royalty to boot) – had his fate sealed in American eyes, word, and deed. He is simply "Black;" no subtleties are permitted.

Obviously this has been the fate of almost every American descendent of African slaves and European slave owners in this nation. There is nothing new here. It is the nature of racism.

But therein lies the irony. Because for Native Hawaiians – in American eyes, word, and deed – any drop of Caucasian blood *diminishes* their claim to native status. In this way Americans decimate and obliterate the native birthright to land that was never ours to claim.

So 'Iokepa Hanalei 'Imaikalani, with a Native Hawaiian father and a mother from Idaho, has been challenged by Americans (never by natives) as somehow less than the Hawaiian ancestry he claims and lives fully. *Kanaka maoli*, the original people, are inclusive. A single drop of native blood and the desire to claim it make you kin.

And yet a day doesn't pass on the Islands when a tourist or a Caucasian resident doesn't ask 'Iokepa, "How much Hawaiian are you?" They are echoing the "blood quantum" measure that malevolent American politicians instituted in Hawai'i in 1921 to disenfranchise a native people and demolish their nation's claim to independence and freedom.

'Iokepa, facing the tactless question and allowing for simple ignorance, answers, "I am Native Hawaiian 100% of the time."

This point was driven home last week. We were served dinner by a waitress in Gainesville, Florida. Lovely, smart, and a good waitress to boot – she shared the face and especially the eyes of 'Iokepa's daughter. We blurted out our take on the similarities and she responded.

"I'm not surprised. My father is full-blooded Cherokee. I'm enrolled in the tribe."

She spoke enthusiastically of her weekends on the reservation: sharing her indigenous culture, observing their ancient rituals. But then she added sadly, "Of course, I can't take part in the ritual because I'm only half."

'Iokepa responded, "If that's enforced, it won't be long before not a single American Indian can participate. Are we going to stop performing ceremonies because someone else says so?"

She nodded knowingly.

So our president is diminished. He is *less than* for being half black. Native Americans and Native Hawaiians are diminished. They are *less than* for being half white. And perhaps that is the

164 / Inette Miller

very purpose of racism: merely an excuse to eliminate those who don't resemble us. It is neither subtle nor consistent, but it has been pretty damned effective.

April 2013

Exclusion

When 'Iokepa wrote the original words on the homepage for our website, he wrote: "If you have a single drop of Native Hawaiian blood, we invite you to join the conversation."

The aboriginal Hawaiians never judged their relationship between one another by the amount of indigenous blood that had – or had not – been diluted by intermarriage. You were Hawaiian even if you were born red-headed, blue-eyed, and aboriginal – if you claimed it, accepted responsibility for it, and lived it.

Since 1921, however, there exists a divisive American government-imposed law measuring "Blood Quantum." It is simply a method of eliminating native claims, and it requires "a fifty-percent blood quantum" to claim native ancestry.

This measurement is something that came to the Islands from elsewhere with the sole intention of politically diminishing the strength-in-numbers of these people. It was, and is, alien to the culture.

So when 'Iokepa stepped up to assume the responsibility for *Huliau–the Return Voyage*, and he put together the words for the website, he was reminding his people of their inheritance, even if the ancestral blood was but a "drop."' He was reminding his people of their need to claim it. He was including the previously disenfranchised.

We could not have foreseen the response from those who are *not* aboriginal Hawaiians to "If you have a single drop of Native Hawaiian blood..."

First, there was the flood of entreaties from people who had lived on these Islands for years. They feared that they were being refused entry to our gatherings – or even worse, were being nudged off the Islands by the very people they loved and supported.

Next, we heard from people across the continental United States and beyond, who were curious, interested, or simply wanted to know more about the Hawaiian people and their beliefs. They too read that their lack of a single drop of Native Hawaiian blood cut them out of the conversation.

Finally, there were the raging emails. These came from people calling us "hypocrites," "racists," and worse because they assumed that they were excluded. "I was born with white skin. Do you love me less? Examine your truth. Your reality keeps us separate."

We were genuinely stunned. We immediately added a second line to the web-page, directly under the offending line and in the same boldface font. "If you have no Hawaiian blood and you want to experience the *Return Voyage* – come."

Then 'Iokepa answered every email.

"My ancestors welcomed each guest to the Islands with open arms, open hands, and open hearts. *Huliau–the Return Voyage* represents a return to what my ancestors lived: inclusion of all parts of creation – human, animal, and element."

In other words, our website was intended to be *welcoming*. First, to the native people who have been disenfranchised by "Blood Quantum" legislation and told that they are no longer Native Hawaiian. Next, to every soul who can find it in his or her heart to value the truth within this ancient culture and the goodness within these indigenous people.

There has been no litmus test for attending our gatherings. I am 'Iokepa's wife and I am an observant Jewish woman from Baltimore. There is love between us, but there is also symbolism, and it is this: Human behavior echoes divinity most starkly in the reach across our differences – in our compassion for the stranger.

'Iokepa and I respect and support one another's often quite alien cultural beliefs. How could we possibly live within this marriage of ours – and exclude strangers from the journey?

December 2007

Outsiders

It appears that, as a culture, we rear our children to fit in. And it breaks our parental hearts at the first sign that they do not. We attempt to protect them from being the last chosen for team kickball; from a lunchbox full of food that no other child would trade up for; from visible orthopedic shoes instead of Adidas; from finding their Valentine box empty.

We live in a culture that has very narrow parameters for difference. Most of us grow up feeling marginal in some way – by virtue of the narrow boundaries of conventional acceptance and the harsh social judgment around those differences.

It was not like that among the *kanaka maoli*. The culture that we celebrate understood no two human beings had the same destiny; no one could dictate another person's path; every life lent a unique contribution to the whole.

'Iokepa says, "Even if a man sat under the coconut tree every day of his life and never lifted a finger to help, at the end of the day the community fed him. There may come a time (or there may not) when he'd stand up and utter the single word that the community needed to hear. No one else could judge that."

These days it seems that our outsiders are speaking their wisdom loud and clear.

Barack Obama is twice cursed as an outsider. He is African American in a nation that still feeds off the collective residue and guilt of slavery. He is not *white*. But neither is he a grandson of slavery; his father was African. He stands outside the dominant Caucasian community and he's marginal, too, among the African American descendants of slaves.

'Iokepa was born and raised in Washington State – not on his native Islands. Unlike most Native Hawaiians, he does not speak pidgin. "I speak Hawaiian, and I speak English." He was born free of the laws that oppressed his culture for almost 150 years. He is decidedly different.

Return Voyage speaks now outside of the Islands across the continental United States. After ten years of preparation, walking and living on each of the Hawaiian Islands, communing with the ancestors – we now speak the aboriginal message as outsiders.

This week the speaking tour landed in Baton Rouge, Louisiana. We were the guests in two homes for two very dynamic gatherings.

In the first, a Jewish woman waxed eloquently about the nature of being reared Jewish in Louisiana – the necessity to fit where you do not into a fervently bible-belt Christian majority. She spoke of the compromises to faith and to self that it demanded.

In the second home, we were guests of first-generation Vietnamese immigrants, who struggle between the pull of their ancient culture and the attraction of their new home.

In the first family I witnessed enhanced creativity, gifted prose, and lively articulation. Within our second family, I saw the invention of ideas, philosophy, and intellectual discovery. In both, there was the transcendent birth of something powerfully new – something different. Each had one foot planted within the dominant culture, and one firmly outside of it. As a result of their heightened perspective, their less confined and clouded frame of reference, they were able to recognize truths that might well be hidden from the mainstream.

Mr. Obama, my husband, this voyage, the delightful Jewish family, and the charming Vietnamese one have reaped the rewards of a life apart. Each carries their soul's gift – intensified by a deep sense of marginality.

'Iokepa said, "Standing on the outside, looking in, we can see and hear more clearly the possible pitfalls of a culture or a people who are buying into something that is not authentic."

Perhaps that's the greatest gift we can offer our children.

March 2008

Boxes

Tell me why it's so much easier for modern men and women to *delineate* – to draw big black lines around our thoughts and our hearts, to categorize, to isolate, to separate – than not. Oddly, this ability has come to pass for intelligent, educated discourse, for a level of sophistication. I suggest that it is none of the above.

Now tell me why aboriginal men and women (the ones whom we tend to dismiss as primitive) saw only unity, only the connections, the relationships, the whole. They could not, in fact, see other than that.

Even as recently as the early 20th century, European higher education was structured and taught in terms of natural relationships. Those formal liberal academies are what we awkwardly cram now into something called *interdisciplinary studies.*

In England, in the 18th century: Darwin (a doctor), Boulton (a manufacturer), Wedgwood (a potter), Watt (the inventor of a steam engine), and Priestly (a preacher) gathered monthly under the full moon to imagine innovation that defied the categories of their expertise. Together they invented; together they transformed England.

Try publishing a book in our current climate. Publishers will scurry to discover the niche – the select group of potential readers who might read this book – and sell to them alone. So *Grandmothers Whisper* becomes only *spiritual* and New Age bookstores are assigned the task of selling it. In that way it is reduced by modern thought to its narrowest denominator, confined to a word that eliminates rather than includes.

My insightful, witty, animated Egyptian friend just published a book. He aims through humor to tear down the walls that separate Arabs and Jews. Moustafa Soliman has encountered this mindset. Ironically, though his work is specifically aimed at bridging differences and making connections, bookstores and potential readers look to impose categories that help them get their heads around his book.

Yet the book business is the smallest part of our national compulsion to show our smarts by how effectively we limit. In college, we sign up for sociology, for physics, for art history – and seldom is the student exposed to the relations between those parts. In the workplace, we are hierarchical; we do not value the unique contributions of the parts. In towns and cities, we divide our social lives by economics, by race, and by education. We do not focus our attention on our concentric circles of dependence on one another. We live as though that dependence does not exist.

We live in a world that is so huge, anonymous, and unrelated that we, quite naturally, search for a niche, a neighborhood, a church, a political party that feels safe – and then we draw big black lines around those folks whom we define as like us, and ignore the rest. This may just be the way that humans deal with massive anonymity, and the fear that accompanies it.

But as a result, we have become very near-sighted. We miss the overlapping circles of dependence on our gardener no less than our dentist, on our electrician no more than our lawyer. We need one another. This is not a pep talk. This is not pie-in-the-sky. This is in no way idealistic.

This is *open your eyes*; take off your blinders; see the world for what it is. It just may be that those big black lines around our minds and our hearts – those boxes – are our self-imposed jail.

February 2013

"I Don't Believe in Organized Religion"

We'd been invited to a Friday evening Shabbat dinner at the home of a Portland Jewish family. It had all the trappings of the ritually kosher home I grew up in.

We lit the candles and said the familiar, traditional Sabbath blessings in Hebrew. Our host, an accomplished professional woman and the mother of three, held her hands over the heads of her teenage sons and prayed that they would grow to be men in the likeness of their forefathers: Abraham, Isaac, and Jacob.

Together we offered gratitude for the loaf of hand-twisted *challah* before us. In all ways, it was the Sabbath of my childhood. 'Iokepa and I were grateful for the invitation, the intelligent company, and the home-cooked meal.

Somewhere in the middle of the Shabbat dinner on that spotless white tablecloth, the husband and father – the owner of a microbrewery, a professional chef, and a transparently good-natured man – confessed. "I don't believe in organized religion."

These are words that 'Iokepa and I hear with surprising frequency. They come across-the-board from men and women reared within Roman Catholic, Protestant, Hindu, Islamic and Jewish traditions.

Most typically, these words seem to be a plea for understanding, a means of demarcation, a way to distinguish between the *organized religion* in which they'd been reared and the *spirituality* that now nurtures them.

These are not people without a belief in the unseen; these are not atheists. They want 'Iokepa – and they want me – to know (with our two viable, culturally-based religions) that they are not us.

They are distancing themselves, not so much from the religion of their birth, as from the ways their religious traditions have failed to practice what they preach – from the lapses.

It isn't the organized religion they are rejecting (though those are certainly the words they use); it is the failure of its adherents to adhere to the fundamental teachings of those religions. It is the compromises of the practitioners that insult, embarrass, and ultimately shame our friends. In sum, it is the hypocrisy.

So to my ears, "I don't believe in organized religion" means: I am sickened by trips to the Torah that are bought by the biggest financial donors to the synagogue; I am horrified by the church covering up child molestation; I reject ministers who live like sultans; I refuse the distortions of Jesus' and Mohamed's words to justify war.

Theirs is an absolutely credible reaction to the false prophets, to the racists who call themselves Christians, to the crooks who secure *aliyah*. Where there has been falsehood, hypocrisy, and outright blasphemy, it has, at times, been difficult to remember the truth.

Yet 'Iokepa's ancestors remind us, "You haven't gone back far enough." Our ancestors, the indigenous peoples from around the world, had to embrace community responsibility and compassion to survive.

The problem is not with the organization of religion – or its authentic origins and teachings. The problem is with the human shortfall. The problem is us – humans who attempt and fail to practice what the originators perfected.

To my eyes, that makes it all the more imperative for us, who've been reared within powerful religious traditions, to seize the reins. It's up to us to steer our congregations and our communities with our example.

Culturally, we have never condoned abandoning a difficult child. We don't believe it wise to run away from our aging parents. Turning our back has seldom healed a wound.

Our lives – the way we live them, far more than the words we speak – are the light for others. The very example of how we place our feet along our singular path is what inspires. We are the models for change, the lantern in the dark, the way to fulfillment of the ideas and the ideals from our traditions and our ancestors.

We are the realization of our "organized religion's" highest aspirations. It is truly selfish to leave the rest of our family alone in their struggle.

Amen.

October 2009

Evangelism

Exactly two years before the Camry met its fate, we crossed the width of the continent in that black Toyota with the gold wheels in four weeks. On that particular crossing: we had dinner with a saintly, eighty-four-year-old Jesuit priest in Portland, Oregon; we had high tea with a Japanese Buddhist. We stayed in the home of the eldest of eight siblings in a Mormon family that traces its roots to the earliest church founders. In Missouri, we broke bread and bared souls with a Unity minister – a woman whose heart is as open as the roads we traversed across Nebraska. In Louisville, Kentucky, we stayed in the home of the man who blew the conch shell that summoned guests to ‘Iokepa and my Hawaiian wedding. In Charleston, West Virginia, we had deep and meaningful conversation with Southern Baptists of the mega-church variety.

Then we were in Baltimore with my Jewish family for my birthday.

Religion makes a difference, culture makes a difference – and well it should. ‘Iokepa Hanalei ‘Īmaikalani would be the last to say otherwise. Our words and our work is about embracing and celebrating those differences.

Our work is not – and never will be – evangelical. We convert no one. We assume that each of us is born with answers of our own, and that those answers require no more than waking up to them – never burying them under someone else's certainties.

Some people encounter 'Iokepa with fear and suspicion. "What *is* this Native Hawaiian culture?" they speak aloud, and the question asserts challenge and doubt. The unspoken question is: "Does it threaten mine?"

The authentic Native Hawaiian culture threatens no one. It does not impose; it does not extract. 'Iokepa says: "You don't have to give up anything. This is about making you more of who you already are."

The Native Hawaiian people have always been (sometimes to their own detriment) about acceptance and inclusion. They were free of judgment. They rejected dominance, sexism, racism. We attempt to model *Return Voyage* on that culture – we aspire to it.

Fear – and its reactive judgment of the stranger – is the infection that was injected by the very folks to whom 'Iokepa's ancestors opened their hands and hearts.

It would have been agreeable if – when those first missionaries arrived in the 1820s; or when the first capitalists came a generation later; or when the New Age gurus arrived more recently – they had accorded the Native Hawaiians the same privilege.

Respect does not seem to be too stringent a requirement.

May 2010

The Task of Youth, the Task of Age

We are nestled, this week, under the brilliantly watermelon-colored Sandia Mountains in Albuquerque, New Mexico.

Nearby, we discovered the weathered lava fields resplendent with American Indian petroglyphs – remarkable symbolic stories that indigenous peoples etched in stone thousands of years ago.

The symbols took us by surprise. Many are identical to those at the mouth of the Wailua River on Kaua'i. These indigenous narratives have certain things in common, but I won't overstate their similarities. This is the desert; our Islands are surrounded by ocean. The stories share common threads, but they are not the same.

It is the point I want to make on the matter of our four-score-if-we-are-blessed human lives: the defining work of the young; the defining work of the elders. We share common threads, but our work is not the same. These differences have been particularly transparent to me on this journey.

Between us, 'Iokepa and I have reared three adult sons and one adult daughter. We are neither unconscious of, nor insensitive to, a young adult's search for individuation.

Quite a number of youthful spiritual seekers have found their way to our gatherings. Barely past adolescence – hardly emancipated from their parental home – these bright-faced young men and women are working overtime to find an elder who will have their answers. They have traveled from one set of indigenous ritual to another, from shaman to guru, from meditation cushion to crystal, from India to Sedona. They sit meditation, they pray, and they retreat from authentic human experience – from trial and error, risk and failure.

"The gift is *life*." 'Iokepa tells them. "The experience of life is in the living it – almost to the edge sometimes."

He says, "Being young is about experiencing. But these young men and women are seeking it, not living it. They're busy looking for someone who has their answers."

To my mothering eyes, these seekers look like terrified children. They are afraid to experience the life they've been handed. They want to skip the trial and error, the fall-down and get-back-up of any authentic life. They want to bypass that exciting messiness and reap the fruits of an elder who has lived, who already has his or her answers.

They are mistaken – and 'Iokepa attempts to turn them back to their own resources, their own potential knowing.

In youth we experience. With age, we digest our experience. When we no longer run so fast, we are freed to contemplate our years of running. But what if we have never run?

These scared young spiritual seekers idealize all that 'Iokepa surrendered at age forty-six to take his walk. Repeatedly, they gush, "You must be so much happier now!" (Without fast cars, fast life, or the pursuit of the dollar.) Their mouths hang open when 'Iokepa answers: "No, I'm not. I loved that life! I loved my cars. I loved my work. I loved going fast. That was *then*. This is now. It's different – not more nor less."

'Iokepa still awakens in the early morning from dreams of the life he surrendered. It is not a yearning. It a *re*-experiencing: the gift of age.

The comedian and actor Redd Foxx said it best: "I don't want to be lying in a hospital bed – dying of nothing."

March 2008

The Face of Geography

It is impossible to travel as 'Iokepa and I do – from Portland, Oregon to Portland, Maine, from Washington State to Washington, D.C. – and not notice the differences. I am not speaking about mountains, oceans, rivers, lakes, prairies, and deserts. It's the human differences – the face of a place. I'm speaking of the angles and planes of the human face – and I am speaking of the human temperament of a place. They are different.

We are at this moment among the cool, reserved New England faces. They are lovely and angular and they are comforting to me.

The cerebral greets me well. These people do not often wave from car windows at strangers walking along the lanes. They don't speak randomly to one another in urban elevators. They seem, to both this Hawaiian man and his Jewish wife, *contained*.

These are not people who are in your face, invading your privacy, or emoting publicly. I speak this with absolutely no judgment. The spaces are soothing for me. For 'Iokepa, I suspect, they are a bit perplexing.

We came to Massachusetts almost directly from Southwest Virginia, where it is virtually impossible to pass a stranger on the street without a conversation that exceeds, by far, a simple greeting. It is 'Iokepa's comfort zone.

There is, in the south, the assumption that humans welcome warmth. The faces are rounder.

I can find no over-arching ethnic reason for the difference. There seems to be an original Scotch-Irish and English blend in both places.

The climates are different, of course. Here, it's cold most months of the year. Caskets sit unburied until spring because the earth won't accept them. *There*, the growing season allows ample time for pumpkins and cantaloupe; the winters are short of excess; summer humidity is over-the-top.

I realize that I'm describing stereotypical Yankee-Dixie differences. We've traveled many car miles and we can (and do) speak with some feeling about the faces and mannerisms of Idaho or Utah, Missouri or Wisconsin.

'Iokepa, himself, carries a billboard of the Hawaiian Islands on his face and in his body; it permeates his emotions. He has wide-spaced eyes in a full, but not fleshy face, cheekbones that cannot be ignored, *kanaka maoli* splayed feet, enormous calves, and brown skin.

But for all the enormous calf and shoulder muscle, these Native Hawaiians are soft. It is how they meet the world: welcoming. Only those natives who've been colored by the occupying peoples on their Islands behave otherwise.

In truth, both 'Iokepa and I savor all these distinctions. In more intimate and penetrating climes, I'm in hiding and 'Iokepa is well-met. In more cerebral and reserved places, he is scratching his head and I'm happily doing what I do – writing alone.

We treasure these differences. We are excited by the adventure of the next unknown place and face. We share with one another an appreciation for diversity of every stripe and wrinkle. And we find ourselves – both of us – in confused opposition to the "all is one" version of reality.

I think we're closer to, "How boring is that?"

We agree to celebrate the excitement of the unexpected dissimilarity. We're forced each day to do that within our own marriage – and so far it's worked out alright.

July 2010

From Sea to Shining Sea

It is nigh on impossible to do justice to the diversity of skin tone or facial feature; occupation or income level; electoral or recreational preference; disposition or mindset among the people we've run headfirst into during these six years on the road. I won't even try. Clearly, we've not traveled these roads alone.

I can tell a single story of an individual man or woman who has tickled, educated, or annoyed me, but to capture the legions we've met in restaurants, gas stations, grocery stores – and at our gatherings – is out of the question.

I am regularly floored by old friends and new who unexpectedly assert connection to Hawai'i or to the Native Hawaiian people. I attempt here a mélange of their stories in hopes that it reveals nothing so much as the depth and breadth of the pleasure and surprises we've experienced on our *Return Voyage.*

. . .

Andy Stokes owns "Stokes General Store" in the tiny town of Front Royal, Virginia, nestled in the Appalachian Mountains. His father owned it before him. He stocks Carhartt workpants, caste-iron frying pans, knives, boots meant for hard wear, and huge wheels of cheese. It is in the true nature of a country store that every discovery feels like an unearthed treasure.

Andy Stokes is a tall, strong, affable man. He's probably closing in on social security age. When he met 'Iokepa last year, this indomitable mountain-of-a-country-man told him the following story:

"Over twenty years ago, I visited Kaua'i for my wedding anniversary. It was the only time in my life I cried when I had to leave someplace."

It was hard to picture this man in tears – and so he repeated it. 'Iokepa had been the only Hawaiian to wander into Stokes General Store in Andy's lifetime. It felt important to tell him this truth.

. . .

I'd been living in Portland, Oregon for some years, when I went to Hawai'i on vacation and met 'Iokepa.

Ten years later we visited Portland, and my husband met my former next-door-neighbor, Tom McAllister.

Tom was an ebullient Oregon historian, journalist, and outdoorsman. He was eighty, blue-eyed, and handsome; he hiked, fished and romped in nature with an energy that would have left a man twenty years younger gasping for breath.

But it was not until we sat down over tea and cookies – 'Iokepa, Tom, and me – that I learned what Tom knew about the *kanaka maoli* in the United States.

We realized, of course, that the kanaka maoli had traveled the Pacific in their state-of-the-art outrigger sailing canoes for thousands of years. But we did not know this.

"The Native Hawaiians were such dependable sailors that they were crucial in keeping early European settlers in the Northwest afloat and alive," he told 'Iokepa.

"The French trappers couldn't swim – and yet they were required to navigate the Columbia River and its tributaries by canoe – so they hired the Hawaiians. When the canoes tipped, the Hawaiians were expected to save the French first, the furs next."

It is a story that 'Iokepa had to visit my old neighborhood to hear.

• • •

We were as far as you can possibly climb north in Minnesota and still be in the United States. We were on an Ojibwa reservation in the town of Grand Portage, when historian and poet Bob SwanSon ascertained that 'Iokepa – so far inland – was retracing the steps of his ancestors.

He wanted to tell us the meaning of *Grand Portage*; and he wanted to tell 'Iokepa exactly how the Native Hawaiians found their way to the Ojibwa people on the shores of Lake Superior.

"From here, we can travel to both the Atlantic and the Pacific Oceans by canoe. We navigated those distances – thousands of miles – on small streams and large rivers, and we had to hand-carry or *portage* our canoe for only twelve miles at any given stretch."

And thus, the people whom the Native Americans called "kanaka-from-the-sea" found their way to the Grand Portage on Lake Superior – and beyond.

• • •

One of my oldest friends is a North Carolinian, a college teacher, and an author of one of the

188 / Inette Miller

bestselling textbooks in America. He is a feet-on-the-ground Southern gentleman.

We keep in close touch by email, and he knew, of course, when I'd begun the difficult process of editing my last book, *Grandmothers Whisper*. But he had never seen a single word or syllable of it.

So it was really quite startling – to both my practical friend and to me – when out-of-the-blue he sent me this email:

"Last night I had a dream in which an editor looks up from your manuscript and says, "No, no, this is not the right way to begin the book."

There was a great deal more dream detail. But the gist of it was that I had buried 'Iokepa's story too deeply into the book, featuring my own upfront.

The email ended: "Okay, Inette, there you have it. I don't know what to make of the dream. I'll let you decide whether it offers a good idea. Having declared my neutrality..."

My initial reaction to my friend's dream was a knee-jerk rejection of his unsolicited advice. I wrote back immediately. "I'm attached to what I already have. My resistance is that this is my memoir, not 'Iokepa's."

Days later, without giving it much thought, the dream editor's critique had become my own, and I made the necessary changes.

In sum, our connections are consistently more than we encounter face-to-face, phone-to-phone, or absorb in books. Assistance from the unknown is there whenever we allow ourselves to trust it.

. . .

Our hosts in Albuquerque planned to take us sightseeing on their day off, a Saturday. They gave us travel guides and several choices. We chose Bandelier National Monument, a cave-dwelling ancient pueblo. It was a two-hour drive. We missed one turn-off and we were delayed.

We were driving down a wide interstate highway in the far right lane. 'Iokepa was driving; I was in the front passenger seat; our hosts sat behind us. A Honda SUV approached immediately to our left.

A dark-haired woman in the back seat of the Honda began pointing aggressively at 'Iokepa. I studiously ignored her. (People often stare or point at his thick silver, mid-back-length hair.) This woman grew more animated.

I thought that perhaps we had a flat tire. 'Iokepa said that we did not. Finally, this woman rolled down her window. 'Iokepa looked over. He recognized her and her driver husband, immediately.

Implausibly, this couple were friends from Kaua'i. We'd eaten dinner in their hillside home just a week before we left the Islands to begin our first speaking tour. We'd had no communication in the intervening six months.

'Iokepa and Dave each slammed on their brakes and pulled to the edge of the highway; all of us leapt from our cars, frantically exchanged hugs, and, of course, stories.

Unknown to us, this couple had accepted jobs that mandated a move from Kaua'i to Santa Fe – months after we'd left the Islands. We swapped phone numbers on the roadside and went on our way.

They called the next day. They insisted that we do a gathering in their new home, "Though we don't know anyone to invite – we're so new here!"

We said: "We can't. We're headed for Flagstaff tomorrow."

But it seems that the ancestors hadn't gone to all that trouble – weren't laughing up their collective sleeves while they moved us around like puppets – for nothing. The next morning we were alerted: the scheduled Arizona gathering had been postponed for a week. Our friends (who didn't know *anyone* to invite in Santa Fe) hosted that gathering in their spacious new home and packed it to capacity.

How could it be anything but easy?

. . .

We were in the heart of hot, dry west Texas, driving east on Interstate 40, perhaps 100 miles outside of Amarillo. We hadn't seen another vehicle for almost an hour.

'Iokepa had shifted to the left lane because the right lane was rutted and worn. We were set on cruise-control at the exact designated speed.

He looked into the rearview mirror and saw a police car flying to catch up to us. "The front of his car was down and he came from nowhere, lights flashing."

We pulled over; my heart was beating out of my chest. This was West Texas; my husband drives without a driver's license. It didn't take much to know how this was going to end: 'Iokepa jailed in this drive-through barren country; me, friendless, trying to figure a way out.

With heart in throat, I watched a strikingly handsome Latino state trooper step out of the patrol car and approach my window. He said: "You were driving in the left lane. In Texas, you can only be in that lane if you're passing."

'Iokepa answered: "There were no cars at all and the lane was smoother."

"May I see your driver's license, registration, and insurance?" I fumbled for the last two items in the glove box. 'Iokepa fished out his computer-generated ID card with photo.

The trooper looked at the homemade ID card and he said: "I've seen Hawaiian driver's licenses before, and they didn't look like this."

I answered: "That's because they were not Native Hawaiian."

'Iokepa said: "I'm a sovereign Hawaiian."

The officer said: "That means you owe no allegiance to the state or nation. What are you doing here?"

'Iokepa said: "I'm a guardian of the aboriginal culture. We're on a speaking tour."

The strapping and dark-eyed young officer asked: "Are you headed to Oklahoma to speak to the Native Americans?"

And so the conversation went: a Texas state trooper, 100 miles outside of Amarillo, who understood sovereignty. *What* were the chances?

Finally, the well-spoken officer asked *me* if I had a driver's license, and I said that I did. He took that, along with 'Iokepa's ID, went to his car, wrote out a warning in 'Iokepa's name with my license number – and sent us on our way.

I was trembling for hours afterwards. 'Iokepa didn't break a sweat. He never for a moment doubted that his grandmothers were along for the ride in Front Royal and in Portland, in Grand Portage, North Carolina, and New Mexico. Why wouldn't they be with us in the desolate brown landscape 100 miles from Amarillo?

May 2013

A Good Laugh

Say the word *spiritual*, and a deathlike solemnity settles over a crowd. Watch a gathering of good folks work overtime to know, feel, or say the right thing. I have watched triathlon competitors swim, bike, and run, and look no less intense or competitive than when I watch spiritual seekers attack their goal.

I have a gentle suggestion: Lighten up.

Yesterday in Detroit, Michigan, twenty-three "spiritual healers" gathered and, despite themselves and their expectations, laughed a great deal.

I introduced 'Iokepa and I said, "When 'Iokepa took this walk of faith, he gave away a great deal of money, a house on a lake, and his seven cars and a hot rod – which *I* happen to think is obscene."

'Iokepa leapt to his feet and answered me. "I loved those cars."

Over the raucous laughter I heard, "How human!"

Later that evening I told the story about how long it took me, the week that 'Iokepa and I met, for him to teach me a very simple notion. 'Iokepa asked me repeatedly at the time, "What's your key?" But it wasn't until our last night together – New Year's Eve, 1997 – that I nailed the simple answer, that I could remember it.

The prescribed answer was: "To ask out loud and then get quiet and listen." Well, at this gathering ten years later, in Detroit, I flubbed it. *Again*, I couldn't remember the answer. I blushed, seriously embarrassed.

'Iokepa leapt off his chair, wrapped his arm around me, and interjected. "Did you see that recent news story about the man who taught his turtle to roll over and shake hands? It took him ten years."

Everyone laughed and loved it. 'Iokepa gave me an affectionate squeeze. My embarrassment dissipated – I laughed with him.

Many spiritual teachers arrive at our doors with *the* answer. Many spiritual seekers expect or demand that answer for the price of admission. Rigid instruction: the one way, the one place, the one teacher who can make it right.

But it is so much easier than that. Our gatherings are thus. We share our personal experiences; maybe a listener finds a word that resonates. In truth, it can never be that serious. Spirituality is human. We humans fumble, blunder, and inadvertently advertise our foibles. Human foibles are funny.

'Iokepa says: "Laughter and spirituality are inseparable. Laughter is a huge part of life – the relief it gives us."

I remember a bookstore owner who attempted to introduce us, and *three* times in a row forgot 'Iokepa's name entirely (despite assistance). Overwhelmed with her failure, Susan said to 'Iokepa: "Now *you* have permission to forget my name."

'Iokepa's retort: "My first three wives were named Susan – I won't forget yours."

The bookstore audience's discomfort dissolved in unrestrained hilarity – and, for the record, there were no "first three wives."

Now in Detroit, an earnest young couple about to embark on what they called a *vigil* to Hawai'i asked 'Iokepa in all solemnity, "What should we bring with us?" Clearly they were contemplating instruments of ritual (feathers, crystals, stones?) – the proper shamanic accoutrements.

Iokepa answered their solemnity with the same. He told them exactly what they would require. "Sunscreen, bathing suit, and beach slippers."

What they didn't need was a teacher who'd inject himself into their experience.

January 2008

Stories Told Around the Fire

The ancestral grandmothers have spoken. 'Iokepa Hanalei 'Īmaikalani and I are on the edge of our seats with excitement. *Huliau–the Return Voyage* is about to shift into an entirely new direction.

The goal remains the same. Within the authentic Native Hawaiian experience lies the answer for a contemporary world tormented by rage, greed, and war. It is ours to seize the ancients' gifts – to return to that which all of us are born knowing. We carry it in our very bones, this memory of another way.

For more than sixteen years now, 'Iokepa has assiduously responded to the direction of his ancestral grandmothers. When in doubt: he has asked; he has *listened* for the answers; he has recognized and then acceded to their guidance. Always, he has offered gratitude.

For the first ten years, 'Iokepa and I were guided to live in tents upon Hawaiian *ka 'āina*. In the manner of the ancients, we surrendered to a life of faith and subsisted without income.

For the next six intense years, we traveled just 5,000 car miles shy of 100,000 around the American continent, speaking the knowledge we'd gleaned from the ancient Hawaiian culture, and sharing our personal story as well.

Now we are to embark on a third phase of this work. We are eagerly anticipating the new direction.

Some things never change. Our surrender is forever. Our walk of faith endures. Always, 'Iokepa and I listen and heed the grandmothers' guidance. They continue to direct our lives.

A Brief History

The Native Hawaiians spoke their lyrical family stories around the open fire. In this way, the community was solidified; the knowledge shared. In this way, the oral traditions remained alive and open to the need for change in a single breath. But for almost two hundred very recent years, powerfully restrictive laws silenced the Native Hawaiian stories entirely.

Around the Fire

In the almost two hundred silent years, there were always whispers. Behind closed doors and away from colonial ears, *some* families insisted on transmission of the truth and the rituals. And because the community stories were silenced, each family held onto a different piece of their heritage. Each family had a sliver of the true history and culture – no one was able to embrace it all. Secrecy, of course, created distortion.

It is time to reclaim that which solidified culture, created harmony, and fostered shared responsibility. It's time to speak the stories.

'Iokepa and I will return home to Hawai'i this summer. We plan to foster the collective cultural sharing of family story that used to be told around the fire.

We anticipate privately encouraging reticent story-holders to come forth. We anticipate locating venues that make full-disclosure culturally appropriate and safe. To this end, we expect to travel the Islands and locate those holders of a family story or two. And finally, we will encourage the public sharing – giving and receiving – in many Island locations over the next years.

The grandmothers have set the parameters. This will never be a means of airing political grievance or pointing fingers and declaring that "my" family stories are the right ones. The purpose of this, the grandmothers tell us, is:

> To claim fully and proudly the heritage that has been forced underground.

> To rebuild a community that has been systematically shamed, by revealing the hidden stories in a face-to-face, welcoming setting.

> To fulfill a 1000-year-old Hawaiian prophecy that foresaw gifting the authentic Native Hawaiian cultural experience to the waiting world.

It was the last Hawaiian King, David Kalakaua, who, under the onslaught of oppressive colonial occupation, dispatched hand-selected emissaries among his people to collect the diminishing stories, chants, and hulas. We intend to follow in that meaningful tradition. It's time to share the flame.

March 2013

95,000 MILES LATER

One of my respected readers asked me: "I get that your lives are about waiting and listening, but I want to know – how do you *feel* about the future?"

It's been almost sixteen years since I agreed to this strange and precipitate odyssey that removed me from both my emotional comfort zone and my physical comforts. These years gave me ample time to understand and accept the absolute limits on what *any* of us know about our future. Oh we plan, and we imagine that we've nailed down what comes next, but last year alone provided me with the extreme example of how much I do not know.

In January of last year, my oldest and dearest friend in the world – a woman who defined grace and selflessness – up and died. In May, I was incapacitated for ten months by a most-definitely-unforeseen car speeding around a curve and into our lives. In November, my healthy and still-singing mother died – two months shy of her 101st birthday.

And yet, that does not begin to define the year – the incredibly talented and good people who entered my life, the exquisite snowfall on the Blue Ridge Mountains, the tent under the Kaua'i coconut palms.

But in truth: I could not – I did not – have a clue much in advance of any one of those enchanting or challenging moments. And so, my friend asks me about the *future*.

I can answer readily for 'Iokepa. This is a man whose most typical response to the unpredictable is: "I'm excited that I *don't* know… excited that I'm on the path." My husband, it appears, lives in a perpetual state of rubbing his hands together in eager anticipation for what life might present.

He *knows* that he is doing what he signed on for. He knows that he won't be let down by the ancestors. He knows that his life of service is directed, purposeful, and full. Occasionally, he is impatient for a larger or quicker result to his labors. But he remembers always his grandmothers' words: "*Ho'omanawanui* – wait in faith."

And yet my friend asked about *me*. I do not typically rub my hands together in excitement at the unknown. But something else has happened in the accumulation of these years. Because I lived those first ten; because I didn't bolt; because the love of this man and his purpose glued me to that oft-times misery – I was, in fact, prepared for what came next.

What came next offered me the deepest satisfaction of my life. In these past six years, I felt used, engaged, and purposeful. This was the destiny I acceded to: my talents and interests so apparently linked to the work we've done. I love speaking; I love writing; I absolutely believe in the *Return Voyage*.

How can I *not* look forward to the unknown future? How can I not see the future in our past? We will continue to disseminate the ancient stories – hopefully in more effective ways, to more numerous and willing ears and hearts. I have no idea how. Hopefully those ears, hearts and hands will pick up the banner and run with it, inspiring others in this unknowable chain of events.

How can I not look forward to this? Because even if everything that we say *appears* to fall on deaf ears and everything we do appears to meet a brick wall – I am no less willing and eager to do it. I have faith that the evidence of change is only occasionally a siren call, and more often a whisper from one ear to another.

August 2013

Mahalo – With Gratitude

Many of these stories were first written over six years, across the interstate highways of America: in hotel rooms, in libraries, in *McDonalds* for goodness sake – anyplace I could snatch a couple hours and free wifi.

But the *book* was written in only two places. Two generous couples offered us the needed solitude for the purpose. On Island Ford Farm in the stunningly beautiful Shenandoah Valley of Virginia, I spent the fall, winter and spring drafting *The Return Voyage*. Our friends Manci and George Orhmstrom gave us the run of those 180 acres. Home on Kaua'i, I spent the summer and fall polishing and editing this book while overlooking the Salt Pans and the blue Pacific. Elizabeth and John Von Krusenstiern, our camping buddies for a dozen years, offered their home and its spectacular view.

My first reader was the accomplished Florida editor, Carol Gaskin. Her suggestions were, without exception, on the money and fully integrated into the final version. My next reader was the gifted Oregon novelist, Maya Muir. She's been my loyal critic for twenty years and knows how to prod me out of my bad habits. My final reader was the iconoclastic Hawai'i playwright, Frank Reilly, who reminded me *again* of the importance of beginnings and endings.

Writer and photographer Hamilton Gregory selected and prepared the photographs for publication – an exercise in discernment. Software designing virtuoso Tom Leonard favored our website with an update for the arrival of the new book.

All of their professional labors on behalf of this book were offered for the price of friendship. I am blessed with my friends.

I thank Sam Conte, who impetuously offered the book's subtitle (during a distant Skype conversation), after we agreed that both *navigation* and *interstates* had too many syllables.

I am particularly grateful for the generous and engaging people who inhabited our lives and inspired these stories during all of these years. Without you, there would have been no Return Voyage.

www.ReturnVoyage.com

You are invited to follow the Ever Changing Page on our website and discover with us what comes next.

CPSIA information can be obtained
at www.ICGtesting.com
Printed in the USA
FFOW04n1453230414
4971FF